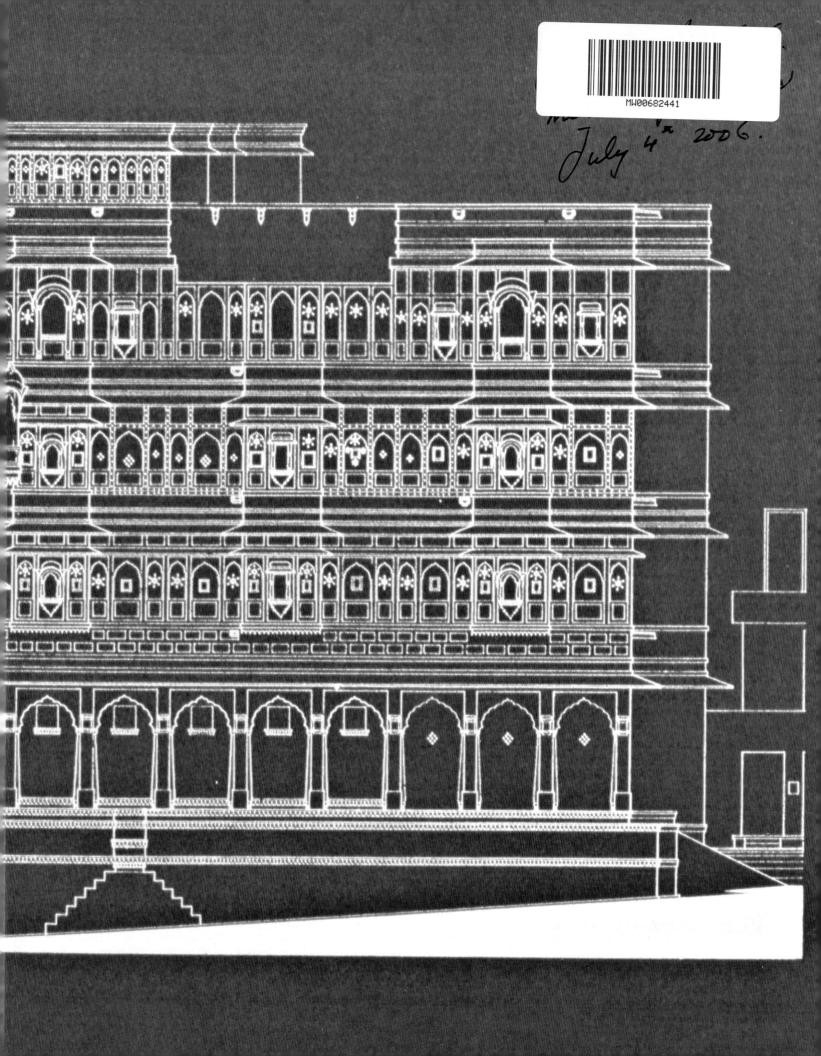

July 4th 2006.

Masterpieces of
Traditional Indian Architecture

ISBN: 81-7436-293-2

Editors: Sujata Pandey, Dipa Chaudhuri
Design: Arati Subramanyam *Layout:* Naresh Mondal
Production: Naresh Nigam.

© **Roli & Janssen BV 2004**
Published in India by Roli Books in arrangement
with Roli & Janssen BV, The Netherlands
M-75 Greater Kailash II (Market)
New Delhi 110 048, India.
Phone: ++91-11-29212271, 29212782
Fax: ++91-11-29217185
E-mail: roli@vsnl.com
Website: rolibooks.com

Printed and bound in Singapore

Masterpieces of Traditional Indian Architecture

Satish Grover

Lustre Press
Roli Books

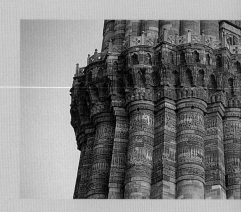

PRECEDING PAGES 2-3: Boulders stand from the near barren hills like natural monolithic sentries of the ruins of Vijayanagar, clad in a variety of colours ranging from gray and brown to pink.

Contents

Introduction
A Perspective View of
Traditional Indian Architecture

The history of architecture in India begins from the time the earliest known wave of immigrants settled, some five thousand years ago, in Sindh, Gujarat and Punjab. They built the cities of the Indus Valley Civilization (about 2000 B.C.) with timber and brick of which evidence still exists.

The Vedic people (1500–800 B.C.) lived in grottos and hamlets made of natural materials such as bamboo and thatch, their forms replicated in stone by later civilizations. The Buddhists built in brick and stone, and carved caves from the second century B.C. to the fifth century A.D.. The Hindus built their religious edifices in stone from the fifth to the fifteenth century A.D.; their secular architecture, built of brick and timber has vanished. In early Hindu architecture the temple was the social and economic focus of a town. The ancient architects followed sacred building rites as prescribed by the *Vaastu Shastra*. The Hindu period gave way to the architecture of Islam (A.D. 1000 –1700), and the Muslims constructed their buildings from the tenth to the seventeenth century A.D. in arcuate stone masonry occasionally using brick.

The architecture of the Indus Valley cities comprised functional, practical buildings in brick set within the rectangular grid of the town plan. The caves of the Buddhists were wonderous caverns of light. These were the *chaityas* of Karle and the viharas of Ajanta cut out of stone cliffs. The timber structures have disappeared but stone and brick structures, such as those at Sanchi and Nalanda, have survived. Hindu domination for over a thousand years climaxed in the building of the great temple clusters of Konark, Modhera and Khajuraho and the vast sprawling temple cities in the south such as Srirangam, Rameshvaram and Madurai. With their knowledge of arcuate masonry the Muslims were able to build large-span structures and engineered glorious mosques, tombs and palaces, culminating in the Taj Mahal.

The architecture of north India was based on political and historical change. The styles that emerged with each successive alteration were distinctively different but inherently Indian in their execution. However, all were influenced by the climate and the local building traditions. Unfortunately few of the structures before the twelfth century have survived the ravages of climate, war and time, yet the region is still rich in the remains from that period. An interesting feature of such architecture is the effortless merging of Hindu and Islamic styles within individual structures, combining the sensuality of Hindu temple architecture with the more austere facets of Islamic architecture.

The techniques for constructing true domes and arches were learnt by the Indian masons from the Muslims after the twelfth century. With the addition of the carving skills of the Hindu craftsmen it became possible to blend the two styles to complement the other and create a style that was Indian in its totality.

From the sixteenth to the eighteenth century the architecture of the Mughal period was designed to awe the viewer and assert the exalted status of their imperial patron. The buildings whether built in red sandstone or marble—symmetry, landscaping and grandeur were some of the common features. The inclusion of fine inlay and latticework, arches, domes and minarets gave these buildings an ethereal grace and offset their massive sizes.

The transmutation of architectural ideas, building materials and structural techniques from one religion to another, and from one region to another is the rich and glorious tradition of Indian architecture.

BELOW:
Carved *Jharoka* with Bengal canopy in the Jaisalmer Fort.

The fourteen architectural monuments and sites celebrated in this volume represent the supreme creations of the many civilizations and religions that prospered in India. Each is nourished by local attributes but transcends the regional to mingle with universal concepts of beauty. These are the cave of Karle, the Stupa at Sanchi, the Kailash Temple at Ellora, the Kandariya Mahadev Temple at Khajuraho, the Dilwara Temple at Mount Abu, the Sun Temple at Konark, the Qutub Minar at Delhi, the Gol Gumbaz at Bijapur and the Taj Mahal at Agra. Also included are the temple town of Madurai, the palaces of Padmanabhapuram and Fatehpur Sikri and the cities of Vijayanagar and Jaisalmer.

The Sanchi complex contains all the structural gestures of Buddhism, the *chaityas*, viharas, the *torana,* the *vedika* and the remains of *lats.* It is the most sanctified of Buddhist sites in the world. Carving of caves was a very unique and developed art form in India. Karle is a huge magical cavern cut out of a cliff side in the shape of a *chaitya* hall. The Kailash Temple is another novel form of building that originated in India. This large temple was built by cutting down a hill slope to leave a huge monolith of a temple in one sculptured building from stone. The Kandariya Mahadev Temple at Khajuraho and the Sun Temple at Konark are magnificent examples of the Indo-Aryan style and represent the best of the Khajuraho and Orissa styles. Dilwara displays the wealth of the Jains in temples that are built entirely in white marble. The Qutub Minar marks the earliest settlement of the Muslims in India; the Gol Gumbaz is the most robust of the regional building styles of the Muslims, and the Taj is the acknowledged masterpiece of the Mughals. Meenakshi in the south is more than a temple; the folds of its *parikramas* transform it into a throbbing temple town of Madurai. Padmanabhapuram and Fatehpur Sikri are exquisite examples of Hindu and Muslim palaces each enriched by its own vocabulary, social nuances and climatic conditions. At Vijayanagar are the ruins of a once grand Hindu city and Jaisalmer is a living fortified city in the desert of Rajasthan.

In totality, these buildings cover the wide spectrum of Indian architecture and town planning in style, religion or location. These are examples of Buddhist, Jain, Hindu and Islamic architecture built with different materials and techniques of construction. From rock-cut caves to stone monoliths to dry and arcuate stone masonry, they represent places of worship, palaces of power, cities to live in and fortresses to defend them all. These masterpieces will never age. Each is the acme of the period to which it belongs.

Karle Cave

Womb of Calm

Time, space and light, the true generators of great architecture, are embedded in the rock-cut caves of Buddhist India. Cave architecture is perhaps the highest symbolic embodiment of Buddhist art and such caves are special abodes inhabited by the gods. For not only are these caves gloriously crafted, they are an architectural space adorned with sculptures that are illumined by a kind of permanent twilight.

The fashioning of architectural form out of living rock has a pivotal role to play in the evolution of creative art in India. Hewn out of hillsides, they are the products of a distinctive technique that does not involve any constructional principles, for the simple reason, that nothing is constructed. The columns are of no structural significance, the arches carry no weight, nor do they counteract any thrust, and the barrel vault is just a shape that supports no load. Thus, no structural accountability is required since no engineering problems arise. The builders could chisel and carve, as they desired to create the space they wished to carve out of the hill.

The earliest example of this craft was the cave of Lomas Rishi, carved by the *Ajivikas* and the Udaygiri and Nagarjuna caves in Orissa. The Lomas Rishi cave resembles the interior of a barrel-shaped vestibule hall attached to a circular cell. The facade is an accurate reproduction of the gable end of a wooden structure laboriously chiselled out of rock.

Wherever caves were fashioned by man they have invariably reproduced the facade and space of the buildings that were conventionally built. The caves of the Buddhists are of prime significance as they transmute their natural architecture into a great art form. One of the most magnificent of these is at Karle, in the Western Ghats, not far from Mumbai. No remnants of conventional building activity in this difficult terrain remain. The monks who ventured here must have had to face the fury of the rains, which lashed down the hillside. The rain fell virtually continually for much of the year and could wash away an entire village without leaving a trace. This made worship around a stupa in the open an unpleasant experience. Under these conditions, the monks could have tried to build conventional halls of worship. Timber was at hand from the surrounding forest and bricks baked in the plains could, though with some difficulty, be hoisted up the steep hillsides. Even so, such a hall would be difficult to maintain and preserve during the unrelenting fury of the monsoons.

FACING PAGE:
Front entrance to the *chaitya* hall of Karle Cave. The cave is a beautifully crafted work of art, an architectural wonder, decorated with sculptures. Time, space and light, the true facilitators of architecture, are enclosed in the rock-cut caves of Buddhist India.

12

It must have registered in the minds of the Buddhist monks that the hills alone could stand up to the annual ravages of the long monsoons. With their desire to make the teachings of the Buddha outlast time itself, they took a cue from the simple caves of the *Ajivikas* and decided to carve out their great sanctuary from the living rock of the immovable hills of Karle. However, this was a feat easier said than done.

The daunting process of carving started around 100 B.C. A few simple caverns, presumably to serve as a kind of site office for the 'resident architect' or 'clerk-of-works', were first carved out. This experimental rock cutting gave the rock carvers a working knowledge of the amygdaloidal and cognate trap formations

ABOVE:
A conjectural cross-section of a *chaitya* hall cut into the rock at Ajanta similar to that at Karle Cave.

that made up the vertical bluffs of the ghats. Their considerable thickness and marked uniformity made them suitable for conducting experimental plans.

In carving out their great halls of worship, the carvers reproduced an exact copy of existing structural *chaitya* halls, halls that contain a stupa, replete with all the details of

the original structure but on a grander spatial scale. The choice of traditional building forms as models for their elaborate caves comes as no surprise. Five hundred years earlier, while creating a facade of the rock-cut tomb of Darius at Nawsh-e-Rustom, the Persians had reproduced completely the elevation of a conventional Persepolis palace. Closer home, the *Ajivikas* had done much the same, although, on a smaller scale. The intention of the monks at Karle was to carve out a familiar *chaitya* hall with an apsidal end to echo the form of a circular stupa, the object of their veneration. The caves are of academic value also for they are visual records of a vanished period of architecture, since they created precise and permanent replicas of the vanished brick, timber and thatch architecture of ancient India.

The hillside at Karle was covered with shrubs and other growth. After clearing it and carving it sufficiently to make it roughly vertical, the gable-end elevation of the structural *chaitya* hall was sketched on the face of the rock wall. Two parallel tunnels were then run to the desired depth and timber wedges were driven vertically into the exposed rock at convenient centres. When moistened, these wedges expanded and dislodged large chunks of stone, which were removed through the mouth of the cave. Once exposed, the desired surface of the rock was chiselled with mere quarter-inch (6mm) chisels and hammers, the tools to final smoothness, before being broken further downwards to avoid the tedious and expensive process of erecting a scaffolding later for the purpose of carrying out polishing. The excavation was technically carried out in this sequence from the ceiling as the sculptors broke downwards. The entire volume of the desired hall thus became a space in stone ready to receive the timber details reminiscent of the structural *chaitya*. Cuts were left for transverse rafters in timber that would complete the composition of the barrel-vault and depict a composite picture of natural rock and inbuilt timber. Some of the timber rafters, protected from the ravages of rain and the heat of the sun have surprisingly survived to date. This process of carving the caves involved three distinct trades—the blasters, the stone carvers and the carpenters. It must have taken years of toil and dedicated labour, with generations of carvers and carpenters following their forbears' trade guided by the rules of their respective guilds, to complete the task.

In the facade of the cave, an exact replica of the front of a traditional timber-and-brick *chaitya* hall, every detail, down to the joints and fastenings of the carpentry

The grand and graceful columns, flanking the stupa at the far end of the magnificent *chaitya* hall. In carving out their great halls of worship, the sculptors reproduced an exact replica of existing structural *chaitya* halls replete with all the details of the original structure, but on a grander spatial scale.

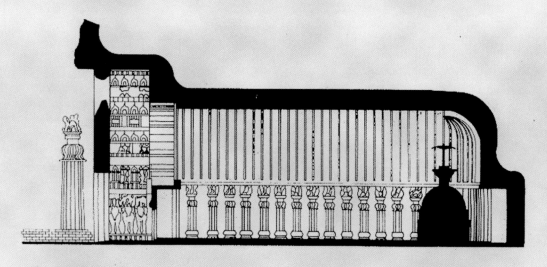

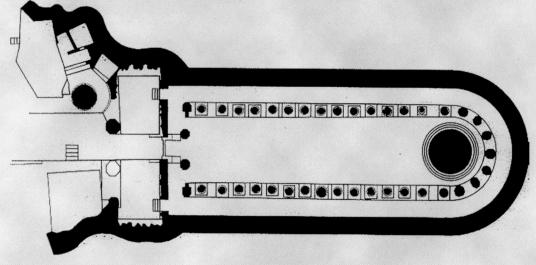

ABOVE:
Elevation and ground plan showing the main *chaitya*
hall at Karle Cave.

RIGHT:
Line drawing of a wooden prototype of a wooden hall
that inspired the Karle Cave. In the facade of the cave,
which is a replica of the front of a traditional timber-
and-brick *chaitya* hall, every detail of the carpentry
construction was reproduced in natural rock.

The Lomas Rishi cave, carved by the *Ajivikas*, a sect of Jain monks, in the Barabar Hills and the Udaygiri and Nagarjuna caves in Orrisa were the first examples of cave architecture in India. The Lomas Rishi cave is similar to the interior of a barrel-shaped entrance hall leading to a round cell, and the exterior is a true copy of the gable end of a timber structure but fashioned out of rock. Taking their cue from the Lomas Rishi cave architecture, the monks at Karle carved out a recognizable *chaitya* hall with a stupa at the end of the hall. The Karle Cave is of academic and visual value, as it is an accurate and enduring duplication of the extinct timber architecture of ancient India.

FACING PAGE:
The full-figured sculpture
of a couple known as
mithuna. The term
mithuna means an
auspicious couple and
these kind of sculptures
can be found on both
Hindu and Buddhist
structures.

construction, were reproduced in natural rock. Apparently those who produced this form of architecture were psychologically still living in the timber age and supplemented the rock cutting work by a substantial amount of attached wooden construction. On the face of the cave are numerous mortice holes for fixing a wooden frontage including timber details of the original wooden facade. The arched entrance portico with window-like arched apertures included stone frameworks of loggias and balconies to receive the wooden infills of grilles and other artefacts, which are obviously missing today. The carpenter's role in the enterprise has been destroyed by time but the main intent of the builders has survived.

The Karle Cave is approached from the Mumbai-Pune highway by ascending some five hundred feet to a large, level platform created by filling the ravine with the debris from the excavations. At the end of this platform stands a fifty-foot high, rather stocky *stambha* or pillar supporting the four lion sculpture, the official symbol of modern India, topped with a chakra. The entire ensemble stands within a square space, bounded by a *vedika*, railing reminiscent of the transition from wood to stone, defining the sacred from the profane. Just behind these guardians looms the facade of the cave, which gives just an inkling of the splendour that it shields within.

Beyond the entrance lies a vestibule, flanked on either side by walls sculpted with tiers of vertically composed gabled arches of different sizes, depicted with railings, balconies, *vedikas,* the square *jaalied* windows and the lotus arches of the gables. At the bottom are unadorned rectangular openings, which seem to descend from high to shallow grottoes in the hillside. These were probably the quarters of the security guards. The light filtering through the large gabled and latticed opening of the cave reveals gentle and abstract compositions while illuminating the entrance chamber. It is one of the most sublime and gentle sculptural compositions of Buddhist art.

Underfoot are two receptacles or pools for water but they stand dry today. Even so a sensation of serene chill seeps through the body as one's bare feet touch the cold stone floor. One feels an extraordinary sense of being inside a womb carved out of rock. The body begins to respond to the peaceful environment as the visitor steps across the threshold into the twilight of the interior space of the *chaitya*. The experience is simply breathtaking! The whole concept of the excavated space could surely be the work only of a heavenly hand. It is impossible not to be moved by the solemn majesty of this unique place of worship, the focus of which is the venerated stupa that looms at the end. Haloed by a hood of light and bathed in luminosity that emanates waves of peace and tranquillity, the message of the Buddha is conveyed in the exactitude of light and space.

When the eyes get accustomed to the quality of the light inside the hall, several

details draw the attention of the viewer. The barrel roof of the cave spans only the nave and ends as flat roofs over stone columns on either side. The pillars are octagonal in shape and depict rural episodes from the Buddha's life. They rise from vase-shaped bases and rest on a square receding pedestal. The subtleties of the details can be described at length, but architectural nuances seem irrelevant in the majestic and exalted aura of the space. The cave dates back to over two millenia, but is alive today and will remain so as long as the hill exists, with its spiritual effulgence preserved for all time. The *chaitya* hall of the first century A.D. at Karle remains an unrivalled wonder of the rock-cutters' art in India.

One walks out of the cave humbled and elated by its promise of tranquillity into the harsh heat of the world outside. The vision of bare blue sky and the blazing sun now seem scorching hot.

Sanchi Stupa

Centred Sublimity

The inhabitants of India between 1500 B.C. and 450 B.C. belonged to two distinctive groups—the semi-tribal population and the Aryans. The more aggressive Aryans had absorbed many of the existing indigenous rituals and from this amalgamation of cultures, a basic caste system gradually emerged—the Brahmans, Kshatriyas, Vaisyas and the Sudras—and were classified as such by virtue of their birth. The Brahmans had created and appropriated for themselves all the rights of performing rituals and sacrifices, which involved great expenditure on the part of the patron. The gods had correspondingly increased in number and each of them had to be pacified to gain peace and prosperity on earth. It was in such an atmosphere that a cataclysmic occasion took place: Gautama, the Buddha, was born.

Prince Siddhartha was born in a Kshatriya family of noble lineage in the sixth century B.C. It is said that the joyful trumpeting of elephants heralded his birth and all the denizens of the jungle celebrated the event with happiness. Prince Siddhartha was born under a tree that came to be symbolized later as the *chattra*, an umbrella of protection.

As Siddhartha grew up in luxury he began to realize the privileges his royal ancestry had conferred upon him. But at the same time he had glimpses of dire poverty during his outings from the palace precincts. The anomaly of his life and that of the wretched and deprived puzzled and disturbed him. Ultimately, at the age of twenty he decided to renounce his princely life to seek a more equitable way that could lead to the contentment of all living beings on earth.

Despite parental pressure, he stood by his resolve and finally left the comforts of royalty to see the world around him as a wandering mendicant. His search had begun and it was destined to be a long, arduous spiritual journey. Gautama spent the rest of his life in search of truth in the course of his voyage to enlightenment. During his search, he visited many places such as Kapilavastu, Lumbini, Sarnath, Vaishali, Gaya, and many more. Having consciously turned away from the elaborate rituals of the Brahmans, he also practised and discarded pure asceticism as the solution. Penance alone did not show him 'the way', neither did renunciation of all pleasures provide him with the answer.

Having reached a dead end of sorts, he now embarked on the last, desperate phase. He was ready to take the ultimate step—starvation unto death. Half way into it, his body shrivelled to mere skin and bone. It was in the course of his self-

ABOVE:
One of the four *toranas* surrounding the Sanchi Stupa. The dome of the Stupa can be seen with a triple *chattri* on top.

imposed starvation in the seclusion of a forest that a voice from a nearby grove was heard saying, 'Son, do not tighten the strings of your instrument so much that they break, and do not leave them so lax that they do not play.'

The advice of a music teacher to his disciple was the truth that Gautama had been seeking and he was blessed with enlightenment. He then decided to preach to save humanity from suffering. The Buddha gave his first sermon at the Deer Park in Sarnath setting in motion the 'Wheel of Law'. He attracted crowds of people with his charismatic personality who listened to his words with rapt attention. He also preached the 'Middle Path' according to which the solution of life's problem did not lie in extreme processes, but in between.

While enunciating the meaning of the 'Middle Path' to his disciples, Gautama Buddha had no idea that he was laying the foundations of a new religion that would later be organized into what the world knows as Buddhism. Buddhism is followed till date, centuries later, by millions of people the world over. Its greatest patron was the Mauryan Emperor, Ashoka the Great. Ashoka had perpetrated the

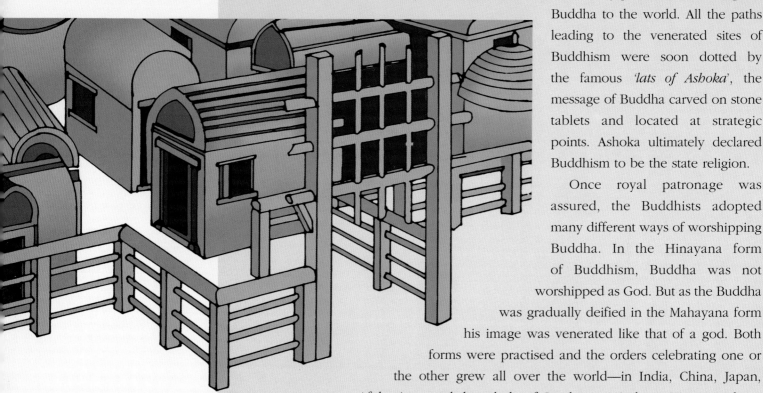

horrendous war of Kalinga, which had unleashed great havoc and devastation all around, leaving thousands dead. He realized the arrogance of his folly and decided to follow the message of non-violence that Buddha had preached. He decided, with all the power at his command, to actively promote the message of Buddha to the world. All the paths leading to the venerated sites of Buddhism were soon dotted by the famous *'lats of Ashoka'*, the message of Buddha carved on stone tablets and located at strategic points. Ashoka ultimately declared Buddhism to be the state religion.

Once royal patronage was assured, the Buddhists adopted many different ways of worshipping Buddha. In the Hinayana form of Buddhism, Buddha was not worshipped as God. But as the Buddha was gradually deified in the Mahayana form his image was venerated like that of a god. Both forms were practised and the orders celebrating one or the other grew all over the world—in India, China, Japan, Afghanistan and the whole of Southeast Asia later. Historians have called Buddha the first great socialist revolutionary of the world. In fact, the spread of Buddhism was a phenomenon of a kind never seen before. But the Brahmans were loath to abandon their control over society and cleverly intrigued to emerge triumphant. A Kshatriya general murdered the last Mauryan king and the Hindus, more organized than before, regained power. They began harassing the Buddhists. In such an intimidating atmosphere the orders of the peaceful Buddhist monks began retiring from the centres of urban power and began to build their new monasteries in more calm and solitary environments.

The largest and most famous of these developed on a hilltop in Sanchi. Today Sanchi is one of the most venerated sites for Buddhists, visited not only by the Buddhists but also by tourists from all over the world. The main stupa is said to contain certain relics of the Buddha that attract pilgrims. The stupa today is seen as a hemispherical mound encased in good quality stone masonry. The mound has, however, been built over many times to acquire its final size and shape. It had also been embellished with many ancillaries at various points in time.

The basic form of the 'Dome of Heaven' had humble beginnings. To start with, it was just a haphazard pile of stones over a burial mound. Over many years it developed from a natural pyramid shape into a hemispherical masonry mound,

ABOVE:
Line drawing representing *torana* and *vedika* enclosing the monks' residential quarters.

FACING PAGE:
Detail of *torana* and *vedika* with the dome of the stupa in the background. The techniques of stone masonry employed in constructing the *toranas* were no doubt as primitive as those used in erecting the railing.

which enshrined some mementos of the Buddha or some other great personage. In fact, its origin as a burial mound was forgotten and it had become instead the 'Dome of Life'. The stupa at Sanchi has come to be recognized as the Great Stupa, not necessarily because it is bigger than any other stupa. In fact, its statistical dimensions (54ft. high and 120ft. in diameter) are modest by current standards. Its greatness lies in its religious significance to Buddhists, as this is where the Buddha's relics are enshrined. The imagination, religious zeal and vigour of the builder as well as the coffers of the mercantile patronage, however, seemed inexhaustible. The designers were soon devising schemes to add new dimensions to the architectural ensemble.

The stupa, at one time covered with shining white lime plaster, is also the architectural focus of an assembly of ruins and buildings scattered around it on the hilltop. The remains of the viharas, where Buddhist monks resided, are on the terraces cut out of the hill above and below the stupa. The places of residence in their starkness reflect rather the inherent austerity of monastic life. These were built as a series of individual cells or dormitories enclosing a rectangular or square roofless court. The open court served all the community facilities including a well for drinking water. The cells, on the other hand, afforded the monks sufficient privacy for the practice of meditation. All the ancillaries were arranged in deference to the location of the Great Stupa, which visually commands the plains around, yet is at a safe distance from the hustle and bustle of the inhabitants who lived in the surrounding plains. On the hilltop, however, there was a hustle and bustle of a different kind, that of architectural experiments and innovations that continued to happen as long as the site remained inhabited by the Buddhist monks.

The circular base of the stupa was surrounded by a high railing that demarcated the profane from the sacred, thus creating a *pradakshina*, circumambulatory path, that took its basic form from the earlier protective timber railing marking the boundary of rural habitation of ancient Hindu villages to protect them from the surrounding jungles. In its new symbolic form, it was now transcribed from the original timber into permanent stone. The building truly replicated the construction of the original, including the tenon and morice joints so common to timber construction. The railing rose to a height of eleven feet and is reminiscent of Stonehenge in its primeval constructional quality. But this railing had a manifest function to perform— that of enclosing a circular path for circumambulation of the monks at the base of the stupa. The techniques of stone masonry employed in constructing the *toranas* were no doubt as primitive as those in erecting the railing. Nevertheless, after erecting the two stone uprights the stonemason

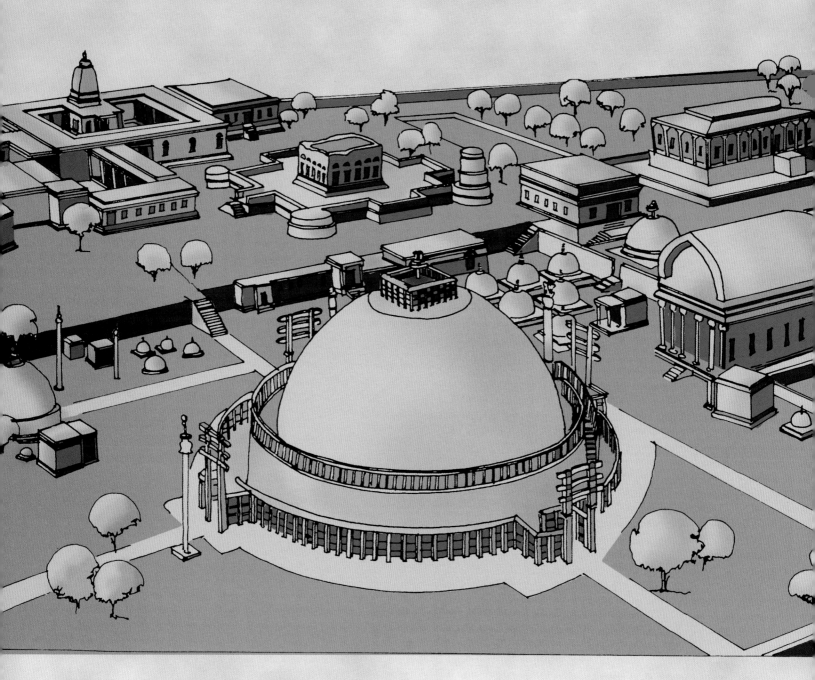

ABOVE:
Drawing of the ground plan of the Sanchi complex, showing the main stupa
and surrrounding buildings.

FACING PAGE:
Map of the stupa and the Sanchi complex.

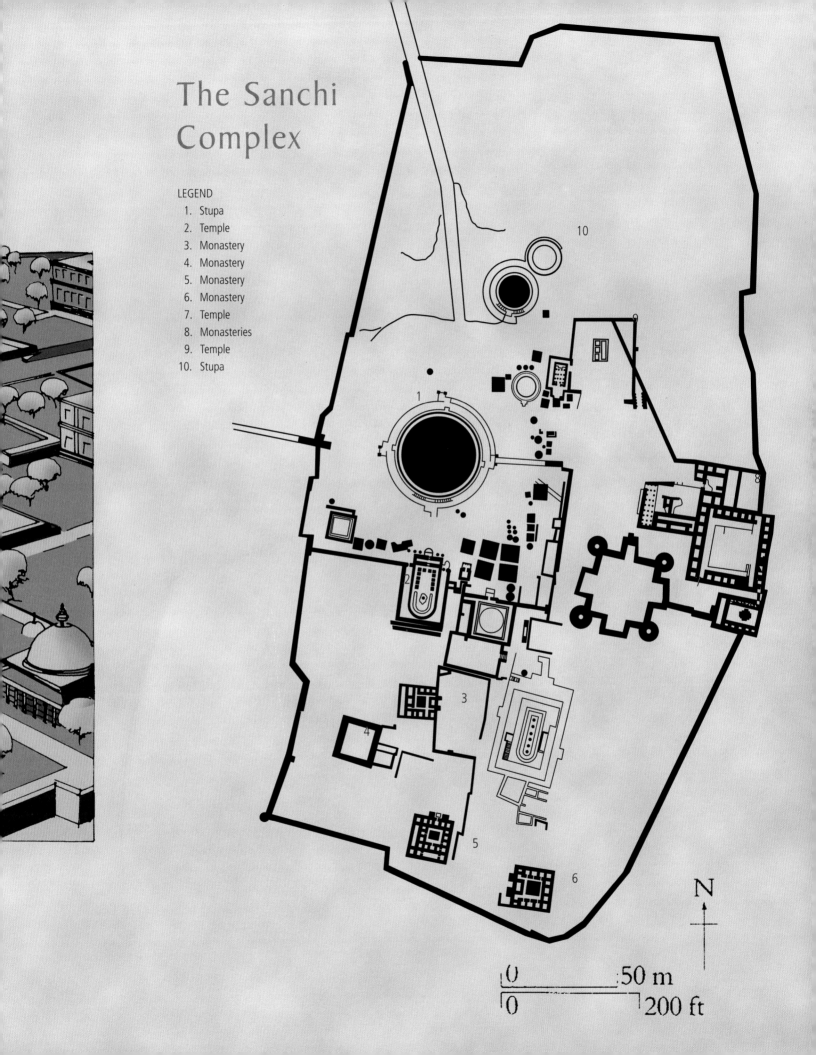

The Sanchi Complex

LEGEND
1. Stupa
2. Temple
3. Monastery
4. Monastery
5. Monastery
6. Monastery
7. Temple
8. Monasteries
9. Temple
10. Stupa

N

| 0 | | 50 m |
| 0 | | 200 ft |

ABOVE:
The Sanchi Stupa in the background of the *torana*. The twenty feet between the stone vertical pillars of the *torana* are spanned by carved stone beams resting firmly and sailing over on either side of the uprights.

realized the futility of cutting mortices and making tenons in stone. Instead, for the first time, he applied the rationale of building with stone and merely spanned the twenty feet between the verticals with curved stone beams resting firm and square and sailing over on either side of the uprights. The horizontal spaces between the beams were then filled in with vertical uprights to create a sort of stone trellis. Each of the cardinal points of the railing are determined by a remarkable gateway or *torana* set away from the railing. They are all attached in such a manner that the result in plan is a composition of a circle and a swastika; indeed a rather unusual composite representing both Hindu and Buddhist symbols. The location of its entrance was staggered from the opening in the railings, so as to ensure privacy for the pilgrim circumambulating the *pradakshina*. The pinnance of the great stupa was flattened to create a square platform surrounded by yet another smaller railing planned as a square, to contain the *chattra*, the symbol of an umbrella that provided relief and succour to all those who came under its symbolic shade.

This form of gateways, including the curvilinear horizontals, had also been inspired by the bamboo village gateways of rural India. By the time the gateways were added on, the craftsmen had learnt the art of stone carving from the Greek artisans who had stayed behind after Alexander the Great's retreat from India. Surprisingly, it were the traditional jewellers of India who responded to this complex new craft and were the most enthusiastic learners as they were used to crafting in miniature all the refineries that women and men needed to bejewel themselves with. Carving stone was only a change in material, and an enlarged scale to work upon. They engraved into the pillars of the *toranas*, scenes of contemporary urban and rural life, *Yakshinis*, the chakra, the elephants and lions—all in a composite celebration of life. They present and recreate in stone, the most enduring scenes of the life and times, myths, legends and everyday joys of the common populace. They are the only physical pictures of a time gone by and the only source of understanding an ancient heritage that has otherwise perished.

Surrounding the stupa in addition to the viharas are assorted clusters of ruins spanning many periods. One is probably a Greek temple dedicated to the fire god, later converted to a *chaitya* hall and from a *chaitya* hall to an early Hindu temple. One wonders what these endless numbers of votive mounds and pillars could be. Each of them is imbued with a distinct lineage and a symbolic value of its own. A congregation of such *chaitya* halls, viharas, votive stupas and the inevitable Ashoka pillars, dispersed on terraces at various levels around the great white stupa, constitute the monastic establishment on the hill of Sanchi. For the Buddhist architect and craftsman, it represented a century of building endeavour, during which he had evolved the essential principles of design of forms that were destined to be the eternal architectural symbols of the religion of Buddha.

However, at the Sanchi hilltop the ensuing architectural style does not result in a cacophony of stone against stone. In the best traditions of the ideas glorifying the 'Middle Path' of the Buddha, Sanchi harmonizes into a peaceful rhythm, a symphony of music set in stone.

BELOW:
One of the buildings with carved columns found in the Sanchi complex.

Kailashnath Temple

Pure Rock Concert

Today the sound of silence that greets you at the great Kailash Temple is as eloquent as the concert of rock cutters that created this magnificent work of art. It is a symphony of forms and rocks, of movement flowing into exquisite movement and rising to a grand crescendo that silences the earth around.

From the snow-covered Himalayas to the arid deserts, from fertile valleys to the plateaus that fall down into a long jagged coastline, India's geography and geology is varied and offered different materials for building through the ages. Since there was an abundant supply of clay from the riverbanks and timber from the forests to use as fuel for baking the bricks, baked brick masonry and timber were used by the Indus Valley Civilization. The Aryans had an aversion to the brick architecture of the Harappans and going back to their agrarian background, used materials like bamboo, timber and thatch. Buddhist monks added their own vocabulary of timber and brick by carving architectural caves out of the rocky hills as everlasting habitable structures. The Gupta period once again saw the use of sun-baked bricks, and introduced dry stone masonry, which continued through the entire medieval and classical periods. Of these varied methods of building, the most extraordinary one was that which created 'rock architecture', a unique form that does not exist anywhere else in the world. Throwing aside all convention its creators fashioned architecture out of virgin rock. They made the task of cutting granite look as simple as that of slicing a slab of butter and as facile as that of the topiary gardener. More akin to sculpture, this ductile form of rock architecture proved to be an extraordinary métier for the Indian genius.

In the seventh century, Narasimhavarman I (A.D. 630-680) decided to test the bravado of the rock cutters and entrusted them with carving models of the various forms of the Hindu temple out of a whale-backed long spur of rock at Mahaballipuram on the southeast coast of India. The craftsmen lived up to their boast and chiselled out seven freestanding monoliths that were christened the 'Seven Pagodas', or raths. Each rath served as a mini model for temple builders in the north and south. The Draupadi Rath was a model of the north Indian temple, topped by a simple thatch roof form; the Arjuna, a perfect and small version of the south Indian *vimana;* Bhima, an elongated barrel-shape derived from the Buddhist *chaitya* hall; and the Dharmaraja, a full-blown form of the south Indian *vimana* type temple. The rock cutters had proved their worth and eminently satisfied the intent of Narasimhavarman.

FACING PAGE:
Stambhas materialize at the base of the hill to mark the modest portal, a most traditional, pyramidal, south Indian gateway to a temple.

After this success, the ambition of the rock cutters knew no bounds and King Krishna I of the Rashtrakuta Dynasty commissioned them to perform similar feats on a more grandiose scale. In a daring leap, they embarked upon a hazardous task and conceived and created the temple of Kailash at Elapura, today known as Ellora, near the Rashtrakuta capital of Kalkhed, about sixty miles from the famous Ajanta caves.

The Kailashnath is the grand realization of a unique human endeavour that defied the obduracy of nature. 'When the gods moving in their aerial cars saw it, they were struck with wonder and constantly thought of it, saying to themselves, "this temple of Shiva must have created itself, for such beauty is not to be found in a work of art."' The admiration of the gods was no exaggeration. The temple was an expression of exalted spiritual emotions, but such a mammoth task could have been possible only through the patronage of a whole dynasty of rulers possessed of unlimited resources.

Today the temple is difficult to discern, as the hillside is dotted with carved caves and protrusions, connected by a craggy pathway. On closer look, a mini *gopuram* and the tops of *stambhas* materialize at the base of the hill to mark the modest portal, a most traditional, pyramidal south Indian gateway to a temple, an unobtrusive entrance to a grand spectacle. Walking through, one is stunned into reverential silence, as if one has entered another world—one of intense spiritual devotion.

The builders of the Kailash knew the quality of the stone they were dealing with and found it ideal for the project at hand. A massive rectangular gorge was first carved out of the black volcanic rock, enclosing a lofty space, engulfed on three sides by soaring cliff-like walls, carved out with immense patience. Near the base of the walls a deep shaded corridor runs like a serpent of darkness a few feet above the ground. It decisively detaches the cliffs from the temple base and the walls of the massive cleavage appear as if suspended in mid-air.

The immense carved out space left a mass of living rock in the centre. This was then shaped down to create a statuesque primordial hill of geometry, which was further trimmed down to create a full-sized *vimana* of the traditional south Indian temple. The entire surface of the *vimana* was adorned with sculpture until the roof became a glowing and plastic statement of its intent. The architectural elements of the *vimana,* such as cornices, pilasters, niches and porticos were carved out in accordance with the calculated precision of the plan, whose three-dimensional proportions were governed by the laws of the *Vaastu Shastra,* the ancient Indian text of the rules on the building arts.

This entire central configuration rests on a 7.6-metre (twenty-five feet) high plinth that lifts it out of the yawning pit surrounding it. In the foreground of the temple rise two huge *stambhas* and a pair of elephants, while the Nandi bull raises its stately horns from the shelter of a tall elegant pavilion—all cut out of

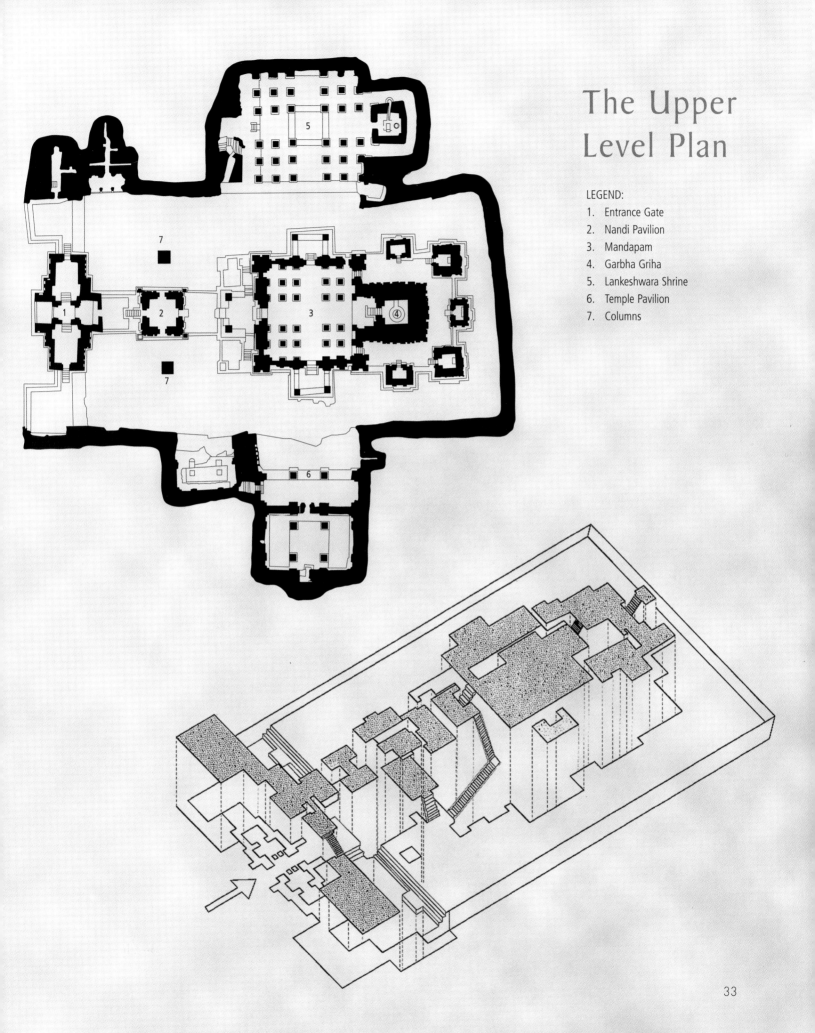

The Upper Level Plan

LEGEND:

1. Entrance Gate
2. Nandi Pavilion
3. Mandapam
4. Garbha Griha
5. Lankeshwara Shrine
6. Temple Pavilion
7. Columns

33

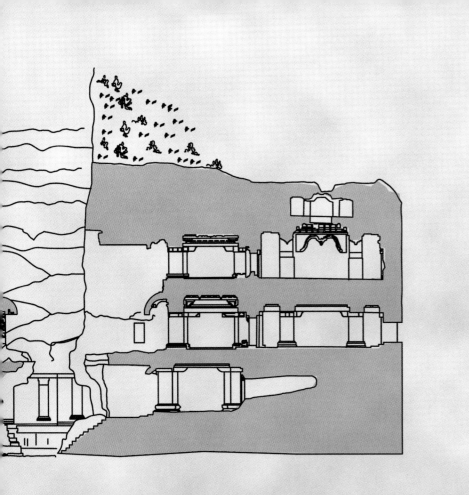

TOP LEFT:
Section of the Kailash
Temple and the
surrounding gorge.

BOTTOM LEFT:
The builders of the
Kailash Temple knew the
quality of stone and
found it ideal for the
project at hand. A
massive rectangular
gorge was first carved
out of the rock,
enclosing a lofty space
enclosed on three sides
by high cliff-like walls. At
the base of the walls a
deep corridor runs a few
feet from the ground,
detaching the cliffs from
the temple base, and the
walls of the massive
cleavage appear as if
suspended in mid-air.

the rock. The flat-roofed mandapam in front of the sanctum seems to be supported on sixteen structurally redundant heavily sculptured columns. The interior of the mandapam is renowned for its lavish sculpture that illustrated the story of the Ramayana for eternity.

The temple today is overwhelmed by the surrounding cliffs, but at one time when it was covered with white gesso plaster, it must have shone out like the snow-capped peaks of its namesake, Mount Kailash in the Himalaya, the mythological earthly abode of Lord Shiva. The sculptures on the plinth, too, were coated with a thin layer of polychrome plaster. No wonder the Muslim invaders of the sixteenth century who saw it in its blazing glory, referred to the temple as the *Rang Mahal*, literally, the 'coloured palace'.

The monumentality of the venture is best described by Murray in *A Handbook to India, Pakistan, Burma and Ceylon*: 'It is estimated that some 200,000 tons (400,000 tons by current estimates) of rock must have been excavated. The back wall of the pit is over 100 feet (30.5 metres) high and the court itself is 276 feet (84 metres) long and 154 feet (47 metres) broad . . . two giant stone elephants . . . a Nandi bull shrine 26 feet (7.9 metres) square and two storeys high. The temple measuring 164 feet (50 metres) from front to back and 109 feet (33.2 metres) from outside to outside of the side porches and rising 96 feet (29.3 metres) above the floor of the court . . . a central hall measuring 57 feet by 55 feet (17.3 x 16.7 metres) and borne by 16 massive columns arranged in four groups of four each . . . a dark shrine 15 square feet (1.4 square metres) inside, with the Ganges and Jamuna as guardians at the door . . . '

All this was conceived by master builders with vision and achieved through the physical ardour of ordinary mortals inspired by sheer faith. It was human power at work, as arms rose and fell to excavate, as the chisel was slanted to sculpt. The years rolled by and the sides of the cliff began to emerge. A generation passed on the tools of its craft to another, whose arms untiringly continued to rise and fall. Time stretched towards eternity until ever so slowly, the deity emerged from the innards of the earth, head first, like the birth of a human being. The process continued until the immense creation emerged out of the unyielding hillside.

It does not matter who started or finished the building of such a venture. What matters is that Kailash was destined to be the great and glorious swansong of rock architecture in India. The enduring glory of the rock cutters' art remains to justify the sentiments of Vishvakarma, the legendary architect of the gods, whose heart, as a poet said, 'failed him when he considered building another like it for how is it possible that I built this except by magic?' Even the architect of the gods shied from attempting such a feat again.

The temple overlooks a vast open space in front—most likely formed by the abundance of rock cut out from the site. The land is crinkled by a layer of stone dust and is devoid of any trees. But it affords a breathtaking panoramic view of the hillside, and is a vast architectural canvas for this unique building venture. The temple is immune to the vagaries of nature, be it the tropical sun or the rain or the thin frost that settles on winter nights. Only when the volcanic heights dissolve in some future cataclysmic event will the shrine of Kailash become the debris for a new civilization.

FACING PAGE:
View of the upper storey mandapam and bridge connecting it to the main temple. The architectural elements of the *vimana* such as cornices, pilasters, niches and porticos were carved out in accordance with the laws of *Vaastu Shastra*, the ancient Indian text on the rules of the building arts.

LEFT:
Aerial view from the cliff behind the Kailashnath Temple. A symphony of forms and rocks, of movement flowing into exquisite movement, rising to a grand crescendo that silences the earth around. The temple is a grand realization of a unique human endeavour that defied the obduracy of nature.

Khajuraho

To God, To Love

The Chandella Rajput rulers of Bundelkhand appear on the scene of Indian history as if out of the blue. From the little that is known about them they were feudatories of the better known Pithora rulers of Kanauj from whom they gained independence to establish their own kingdom. They did not leave their mark on history, neither having played a role in court intrigues nor having indulged in wars of any consequence. Thus their rise to power seems to have gone unnoticed. However, when Khajuraho was discovered, it made an indelible impact on the architectural history of India. The great temples the Chandellas built, over a brief period of power, are today considered the high mark of Hindu temple architecture in north India.

A British Captain in the army who was traversing the plains of Madhya Pradesh in 1838 discovered Khajuraho quite by chance. At the suggestion of his *palaki* bearers he made a detour to rest in Khajuraho village—a name derived from *khajur*, the date palm trees that flourish there. It was by providence that the Captain discovered a group of sixteen temples, that were probably, 'the first aggregate number of temples, congregated in one place to be met within India, that are within a stone's throw of one another.' Today, they are celebrated as the Temples of Khajuraho and under their shadow are held dance and music recitals that draw people from around the world, enhancing the monumental quality of this priceless site. The modern world recognized the uniqueness of the temple art and UNESCO declared it a World Heritage Site.

The Chandella kings of Khajuraho, located in the Chhattisgarh district of Central India, seemed to have had a premonition that they would not rule over their territory; and their fears were well founded as they ruled for just about a century or so. Their reign was like the brilliant flash of a meteorite blazing across the sky. During this dazzling phase, apart from building many public welfare engineering projects, such as reservoirs, dams and water tanks, they created the most exquisite temples—at a feverish speed.

At one time the temples must have been part of a bustling and prosperous city or town. The rulers could afford craftsmen and architects of the highest skill. Today the city has disappeared in totality, leaving behind—what was until not very long ago—just a sleepy village and a scattered group of temples which collectively created their own unique style, known as the 'Khajuraho style'. The architects of the Chandella kings seemed to have worked breathlessly in tandem

ABOVE:
The Kandariya Mahadev Temple at Khajuraho stands on a plinth that raises it above ground level. The discovery of Khajuraho made an indelible impact on the architectural history of India. The great temples are today considered the high mark of Hindu temple architecture in north India.

with their rulers, as if aware, that their fame would be brief. And so in Khajuraho, within a range of just two square kilometres, is an architectural concert frozen in a frame, in which the birth of a note rose to a crescendo, and its sudden thundering conclusion took place within a quick passage of time.

It must have been an amazingly frenzied century of creativity during which the labour of love gave rise to these temples. The temples that rose grandly out of barren, flat and dusty countryside seem like some primordial image of the immortal Himalayan mountain ranges, home of the sages and the great gods of Indian mythology. Seen in their entirety they reveal the linear growth of an idea, its maturing with age and its ultimate fruition, in terms of planning, architecture, craftsmanship, precision and, what is most apparent, highly dexterous sculptural skills.

The elements of the idea were born early in the tenth century. A simple temple was constructed, consisting merely of a small, flat-topped cubic *garbh griha* to house the God and an attached veranda for the worshippers. In the next effort, the *garbh griha* was given architectural eminence and topped with a tall tapering roof termed as the *shikhara,* literally, the peak. In a later attempt, the veranda was enlarged into a large square space, called a mandapam. A pyramidal form derived from a treabeate structural technology that involved converting a

41

The Kandariya Mahadev Temple

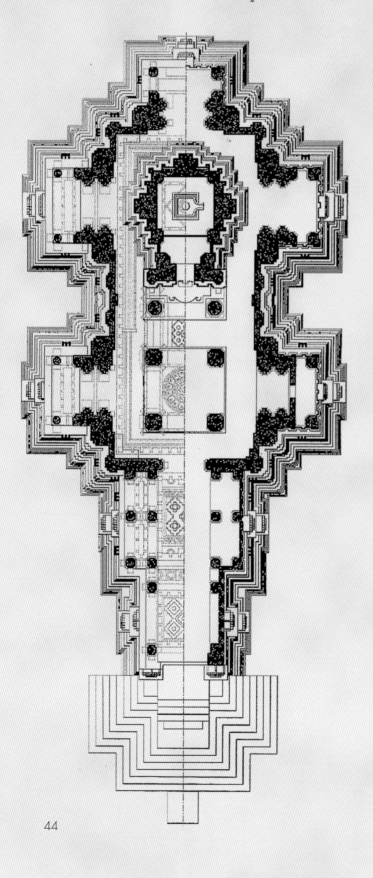

square into an octagon by elementary bracketing that roofed the mandapam. The basic building skills and the architectural ideas of the master builders were obviously appreciated by the Chandella rulers, who encouraged these efforts with further endowments from an obviously prosperous economy.

The builders were buoyant, assured by the confidence placed in them by their patrons. They attached to their earlier attempt a hall for devotees to assemble and sing or dance. A square entrance portico, defined by surrounding stone benches for pilgrims to rest awhile, preceded this. The concept was further extended by linearly attaching another portico called the *ardh* mandapam in the next endeavour. The evolution started at the Ghantai Temple and proceeded through the Javeri, the Chatarbhuj and the Surya Chitragupta Temples. But the Laxmana, the Parsavanatha and the Vishwanatha Temples are the most elaborate of all the examples and indicate the climax at Khajuraho.

The pinnacle of the growth was the Kandariya Mahadev Temple devoted to Lord Shiva, the presiding deity of Khajuraho. The concert that started many years ago reached a crescendo that was played out to a resounding peak. It was the most magnificent in size and built and crafted with the greatest of engineering skills. It was the high note of the concert. Even now one thousand years after the musicians of the concert are gone, the architectural notes resound in the skyline and ring like a bell that emits an endless sound, even before it is struck.

The *shikharas* of the temple make one dizzy with their soaring height. The graceful peak line of this temple was achieved by the subtle linearity of the main parabolic curve. The contours are taut and the tempo of the lines is accelerated as they mount upwards. The refinement is obtained by the design and distribution of the *urusringas*—

LEFT:
A section
of the Kandariya
Mahadev Temple
wall showing
details of
sculptures which
seem as if
craftsmen from
another world
carved them,
a world of
sensuous mystery
where sober
reality is
unknown.

45

The Kandariya
Mahadev Temple

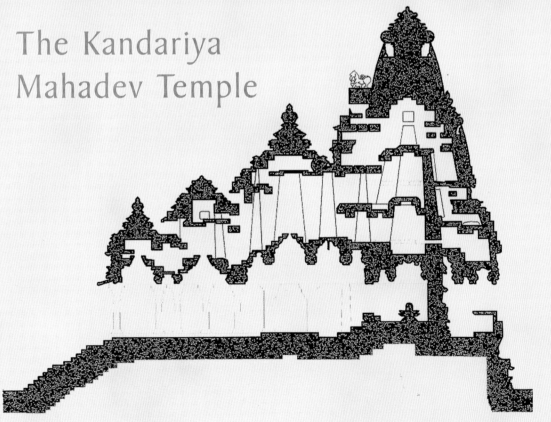

ABOVE:
Fine carving of a cornice
of a *shikhara* of the
Kandariya Mahadev
Temple.

FACING PAGE:
The majesty of the
Kandariya Mahadev
Temple, rising grandly
out of the barren, flat
and dusty countryside,
like a primordial image
of the immortal
Himalayan mountain
ranges.

shikharas in relief, which were superimposed deftly on the sides to break up the mass of the main peak into many smaller surrounding peaks. The manner in which the craftsmen played and even juggled with these elements with mathematical precision, to shape the spire over the *garbh griha* proved that they were masters in the art. The quoins of each attached *urusringas* were continued until the next miniature one appeared at the junction of the quoins in order to cushion the drop of the *shikhara*, marking the merger of the top and the well-defined horizontality of the base. Each of the attached *shikharas* is repeated five times in descending size, resulting in a harmonious, graceful and robust outline to the volume—all this is the result of long apprenticeship by generations of builders at Khajuraho.

The Kandariya Mahadev Temple is the 'Everest' of the 'mountain ranges' at Khajuraho. It rises 116 feet above the platform level and the *shikhara* is the apex of the immensity of a compact mountain range. The sacred space inside was like a cave carved out of these mountains, culminating in the mysterious and eternally dark *garbh griha*. The entrance vestibule and the mandapams are parts of a strictly precise and harmonious entity. Interior compartments are rhythmically grouped like a team of ballet dancers that is transformed into an architectural plain with rare elegance. The entire scheme is fabricated from the geometrical rules of the *Vaastu Shastra*. No liberties are taken with its trustworthy and reliable instructions.

A plain, pillared aisle stretches out to receive the visitor at the top of the flight of steps, leading to an open mandapam supported on four central columns. The dark cubic cella is approached via the *antralaya* or anteroom, immediately behind, which lies the cubic *garbh griha*. An enclosing wall circumscribes the unlit part of the temple. The elegant skyline of the body of the temple was a logical outcome of such a precisely delineated plan. The profile of the shallow pyramidal roofs over the mandapams ascends and descends gracefully towards the apex of the *shikhara*, centrally located over the holy cella.

The heat of the plains, however, seemed to have lit the sculptors' torch with a strange burning, and obviously with the blessings of their mentors, they began chiselling into the walls and *urusringas* vivid scenes of sexual joy. It almost seems as if craftsmen from another world carved them, a world of sensuous mystery where sober reality is unknown.

This candid display of erotic love on the walls of the Hindu house of God remains a mystery that visitors must answer on their own. To a certain degree, erotic or at least highly suggestive sculpture and painting are common in Indian temples, almost from the earliest times. They can be passed off as expressions of the Indian craftsman's love for life in all its aspects. But the erotica of Khajuraho, is not restricted merely to the amorous embraces of copulation between man and woman, but what in contemporary perception would be described as free

FACING PAGE:
Details of sculptures from the
Kandariya Mahadev Temple.

48

group sex, that which a conservative interpretation would label as perverse and degenerate. Khajuraho was in effect a 'cinema bleu' of the most sophisticated kind.

The fantastic variety and exuberance of such erotica is unimaginable. In addition to scenes of sexual intercourse, all the nuances and fetishes of sex, are performed in wondrous acrobatic contortions, richly covering the temple on all sides in sculptural panel after panel. To the devout defenders of the moral purity of Hindu faith 'this evil erotica' is purposefully perpetrated to ward off the 'evil eye' or is a device to highlight the contrast between the evil outside and the purity of the inner sanctum; the walls of which are bereft of the sculptors' skills. Some believe that various tribal tantric rites, some of which were absorbed into Hindu mythology, inspired the erotica. But Freudian thinkers would analyse this erotic display as the manifestation of a society undergoing a monumental catharsis, to purify itself of all its sins. A few would probably agree that pure erotica was only a logical conclusion to the theme of love—the ultimate union between man and his maker. However, whatever your judgment is, underlying these sensuous stones is the most fundamental of Hindu tenets—'discover yourself'—whichever way you like. Are the sculptors of Khajuraho showing one way? The viewer is free to decide.

Sun Temple

Chariot of Fire

Among the principal Vedic deities, Surya, the Sun God, held a place of pride. In course of time, Surya was absorbed into the Hindu pantheon of deities, with a strong cult-like following, and became part of the organized Hindu religion as practised in the north of the country. Oddly enough, there are just a handful of temples devoted to Surya, and these are mainly located in the north, west and east of India. There is a Sun Temple in the north in Martand (Kashmir), one at Modhera in the west, one in the northwest in Orissa. However, the last and most splendid of all the Sun Temples is the one located in the east in Konark.

Martand, a land of a harsh climate, is today a dilapidated ruin of a once grand temple, whose intrinsic beauty can be seen in its assembly of trefoil arches and elegant gable roofs. The Modhera Temple overlooks a huge rectangular water tank surrounded by an elaborate geometrical maze of ghats. The entrance to the temple was through a free standing *torana, a* decorated gateway, which led to the columned mandapam. The *shikhara*, or spire, of the temple was destroyed in a devastating earthquake centuries ago. At Orissa, the Sun Temple is a simple folk structure distinguished only by the circular columns of the entrance portico that rise directly from the ground, a rarity in Hindu temples.

A befitting commemoration of the might of the Sun God that rises from the east was left, however, to the eastern region itself to celebrate. It was none other than King Narshimadeva in the thirteenth century who accepted the challenge and took on the responsibility of building a colossal, magnificent edifice at Konark.

The Sun Temple at Konark is the climax of a rich building tradition spanning eight hundred years and culminating in the Lingaraja Temple at Bhubaneswar and the Jagannath Temple at Puri in the thirteenth century. These were the largest of all the temples in each of the two cities. The Lingaraja Temple at Bhubaneswar was initially planned only as a *deul*, or inner cella, and a *jagmohan*, hall of worship, each of gigantic proportions. As the Brahman system of worship expanded, so did the temple complex. Halls to accommodate the new rituals were erected along

the main axis of the temple—the *Bhog Mandir*, a hall for the gods to bless the food offered by donors for distribution to the destitute; and the *Nat Mandir* for the dance performance by *devadasis*, handmaidens of the gods, who danced the *Odissi*, a classical dance form indigenous to Orissa, for the gods.

The architectural development of Jagannath Temple at Puri is virtually the same as that of the Lingaraja Temple. However, to ease the pressure of crowds at the Jagannath Temple, the likeness of an image of the presiding deity was annually taken out of the *deul*. This was mounted on a huge rath, and carried through the city in procession. This signified that the god had deigned to come down to the people so that devotees of each caste could worship him. This gigantic wooden chariot mounted on a number of large wheels had to be pulled by thousands of stout men and, once in motion, the rath was difficult to stop.

In contrast, the Konark Temple for the Sun God is an allegoric stone vision of the deity as described in the *Rig Veda*. The builders of Konark's Sun Temple envisaged the chariot as if time's wings had been attached to it to fly the Sun God from east to west, charting out an aerial route for the god's celestial car. The god rises in the morning to herald the beginning of the day and rides across the

ABOVE:
The Konark Temple for the Sun God is an allegoric stone vision of the Sun God
as described in the *Rig Veda*.

heavens in a chariot drawn by seven horses. He is ensconced in the *deul* of the temple and is pulled by the *jagmohan*, here depicted as a flying chariot. In front of the *jagmohan* is a wide flight of steps bound on either side by richly caparisoned steeds regally harnessed, rearing and straining as they strive to drag the great bulk of the chariot along and fly it over the flat roofed *Nat Mandir* in front. The horses are flanked by two gigantic, trumpeting elephants curiously carrying human torsos entwined within their trunks. The heavily sculptured wheels at the base of the *jagmohan* facilitate the vision of motion generated by the horses. The entire stone temple seems to stand on a runway waiting for the take-off signal from a control tower, a gloriously breathtaking depiction of the rising sun! According to legend, once the god unharnesses the seven legendary horses he sends the signal for night to cover the earth. It is indeed the most grand and eloquent tribute to the Sun God in India.

The irony of the Sun Temple at Konark is that the god who stood tall in the *deul* fell soon after or perhaps even before the temple's completion. Some believe that this inauspicious accident occurred because the walls of the temple were sculpted with innumerable and, at times, larger-than-life images of naked couples indulging in joyous copulation.

These images, each created by master sculptors, render an exuberant erotica of 'the most immoral kind'. Larger-than-life couples immersed in the sensual bliss of union portray sex and its blissful aspect. The faces of the participants in the love scenes are graciously depicted in a state of complete bliss and joy, immediately transforming the lurid into a great work of art. Elegance and beauty lift them from the realm of the low and vulgar. However, diehard moralists concluded from this erotic display that immorality had crept into the courtly life of the kings and the religious life of the priests, and this is what led the gods to destroy the *deul*.

A more realistic interpretation of the collapse of the *deul* ascribes it to technical reasons of statics, stability and construction. While a genius had conceived the architectural fantasy that the temple is, its colossal grandeur was beyond the technical means of the builders. The immense size envisaged was perhaps too large for the technological expertise of the times. The engineers were apparently so fascinated by the architectural imagery of the project that they took on more than they could chew. The huge *shikhara* of the *deul* collapsed, but the part representing the motions of the sun in a chariot exists even seven hundred years after it was built. 'It is what moves that stays' as an ancient poet had predicted. While the part representing motion stayed, what stood tall, fell. Nevertheless, what stands today is a massive 'mobile' stone tableau that amazes one by the gigantic size of its conception. The *deul* housing the god rose to a height of 225 feet. The chariot-like *jagmohan* measures more than 50 feet square at the base and rises 100 feet to the base of the pyramidical roof over it. It was termed the 'Black Pagoda' by seafarers who used it as a navigational aid and, according to a legend, a lodestone was mounted at the apex of the pyramid that allured the sailors either to a safe haven or to disaster.

Unfortunately, visitors cannot enter this huge *jagmohan* today and can only visualize the vast space inside because of a grave mistake that was committed—attempting to carry the architraves of the temple to a museum in Kolkata without understanding their importance to the structural concept. This attempt, however, failed in its ultimate aim in spite of available modern technology. Thereafter, a massive feat of modern engineering was needed to hold up the roof, which

The Surya Temple

LEGEND
1. Sanctum
2. Mandapam
3. Dance Pavilion
4. Mayadevi Temple
5. Vaishnava Temple
6. Horses
7. Elephants

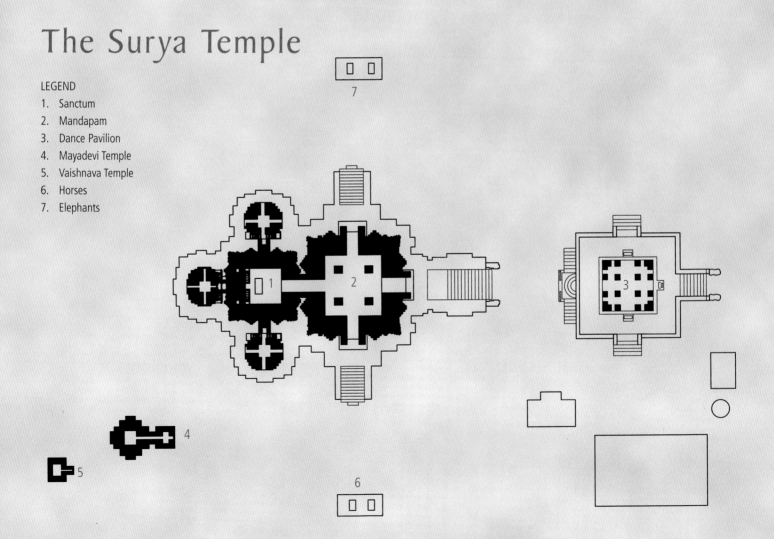

LEFT:
A panel of sculpture
from Konark.

FACING PAGE:
Plan of the Sun Temple,
Konark.

began to show signs of collapse. Even the iron beams that were used in its construction—for the first time in a temple—did not prove strong enough. Some hundred years ago efforts to stall it caving in were made by building extra supports and by replacing its old but un-rusted iron beams with modern steel beams. This attempt too proved futile and, as a last resort, its interior was sealed with rubble and sand to prevent an imminent collapse of the structure.

Fortunately, as in all Hindu temples, only the external facade of the temple is the recipient of the sculptors' skills. What we can see today on the outer walls of the *jagmohan* is frieze upon frieze of mythological sculptures. The wheels of the chariot are sculpted with elaborate geometric patterns as well as human figures in the central meeting point of the ten spokes of each of the twenty-four wheels. The walls of the *jagmohan* are embellished, apart from erotica, with more

sanguine sculptures of gods and goddess on which more care has been endowed than on the erotica. The huge cornices of the pyramidical *jagmohan,* could support larger-than-life, freestanding, full-bodied sculptures, which could be viewed from all around. These are statuesque figures of musicians, dancers and drummers that celebrate the rising of the Sun God to entertain him during his mythical journey around the earth.

The entire planning concept of the spectacular temple is devised out of the perfectly square plans of the *deul*, the *jagmohan* and the *Nat Mandir* and their precise geometric subdivisions. The main temple and the *deuls* of four accompanying deities at the corners of the platform are all laid out on the ground according to a strict regimen. The mathematics of the vertical and horizontal dimensions follow the dictates of the *Vaastu Shastra*, the ancient treatise on the art and science of building, which are basic to the design of all ancient temples in India. The entire plan of the temple was defined by walls enclosing a courtyard that measures 865' x 540' and gives an indication of the gigantic size of the temple. It was approached through three entrance gateways in the centres of the east, north and south sides, which have succumbed to the ravages of the saline sea wind and are probably buried in the sand dunes that stretch out as far as the sea.

The magnificence of the temple was such that even a heathen, on seeing the Konark Temple wrote, 'those whose judgment is critical and are difficult to please also stand amazed at the sight.' The heathen was Abu'l Fazl, the official historian of the Mughal court, who recited the highlights of his journeys in India to Akbar. He must have seen, but discreetly omitted any reference to the works of erotica 'on winged wheels' to his emperor.

The Sun God, however, mischievously takes them all along—the musicians, the singers, the dancers, cymbal players and drummers, not forgetting the licentious lovers, to keep him company on his transcendental journey of light and fire across the earth.

Dilwara Temple

Dazzling Wealth

Viewed from the arid plains below, the hill of Abu appears to be crowned by a glowing mass of white. Appearing almost like a craggy snow-capped mound from the base, this glowing mass is actually a skyline of *shikharas*, domes and colonnades, all built of radiant white marble. This stunning cluster of temples does not belong to yet another Hindu city but is a group of Jain temples that forms a distinct style of temple architecture which is Buddhist in its ideology, Hindu in its architectural form with some Islamic elements as well.

The *Jaina* or Jain community that built these temples frequently pulled down their old and decaying buildings to replace them with new ones. In doing so, they left hardly any trace of their earlier style once the new structure came up. The basic architectural form of the temples that stands out today is adapted from Hindu physical features such as the mandapam and *shikhara*. Although the mandapam in front is roofed over by a dome, the walls of the courtyard surrounding the main shrine contain a series of niches. These are filled by identical images of the austere *Jinas*, teachers, seated in a cross-legged posture.

For some reason the Jains never created new architectural forms to suit their own functional needs. They only altered the functions of the mandapam and the *shikhara* of Hindu temples to suit their ideology. Unlike the Hindus, the Jains do not worship a pantheon of gods nor do they sing songs of praise or dance to please the deity. They concentrate all religious rituals in obeisance to Mahavira, 'literally' the conqueror or victorious one. Mahavira is their only god and is revered as a cold, white, forbidding image with blazing red, bloodshot eyes that keep a wary watch on the activities of his followers.

Dating back to about three thousand years, Jainism was founded by Mahavira who was considered the last recognized Jain leader, much like Mohammed who was the last in a series of prophets. Mahavira enunciated a doctrine that was formulated by a mythical succession of earlier teachers. Of them, were twenty-three known as *Jinas* or the *Tirthankaras*. Mahavira was the twenty-fourth and was acknowledged as the greatest of them all. Buddhism may have overshadowed Jainism in its early period, yet it remained a powerful presence and found its own rightful place again around the fifth century A.D.

Mahavira's teachings echo the theory of non-violence propounded by his contemporary Gautama Buddha in the fifth century B.C. However, there are

FACING PAGE:
Sculpted figures from the ceiling culminate at the apex in a goup of pendant-like festoons of foliage made of transparent white marble suspended from a high tree in a forest. The ground axis of the entrance culminates in a stern looking statue of the Mahavira in an open cell at the end of it.

several twists and mythological additions in the theology of the Jains that distinguish it from Buddhism. Its visual traditions can be traced back to the concept of the mythical churning of the ocean by using Mount Meru, that was regarded as the beginning of creation. Indeed, it draws most of its theoretical architectural parameters from this myth.

The Jains chose the same kind of building sites as the Buddhists had, and built their temple cities on isolated hilltops far from the main highways. The hillocks were designated as 'mountains of immortality', and became sites for picturesque temple towns, such as those in the Palitana, Girnar and Shatranjuya Hills. These isolated holy hills are adorned by a crown of 'eternal *chaityas*', as envisioned by the Jains. The monastic community, thus in a way shunned day-to-day practical life and its problems. Yet, although this suited the orthodox, what of the commoner seeking to find a livelihood?

Non-violence, the essence of Mahavira's preaching, was taken by the Jain clergy to its theoretically logical end but it leads to a somewhat absurd conclusion: namely, that no living being must be killed by a Jain, and their definition of 'no living being' was meant to be taken literally. For in their endangered list of living beings were not only humans and animals but also the world of insects, down to the tiniest ant. To harm even these was considered reprehensible, and for the orthodox followers to kill them was to commit the equivalent of a cosmic sin. The Jain monks wore a fine gauze mask, so as not to breathe in and kill any live organism. When they walked, they carried a broom with them to clear away ants and other insects lest they get crushed under their feet. All this is nothing short of a monomania and one wonders if Mahavira really postulated such extremes. These notions were probably created by Jain monks to carve out an independent identity for their unique form of worship.

This eventually led to an intriguing situation. Adherence to the dictates of Mahavira forced his disciples to follow a lifestyle which was unique to the community. They realized that their founder's dictates followed in a strict sense would be difficult to adhere to in practical life. They had to find a way out for carrying out their everyday life. Else, they could not be rulers or administrators who would have to use torture and order death as a routine punishment for criminals, nor be involved in any kind of animal husbandry nor in tilling the soil, for that would lead to the death of countless worms and insects. They realized that under such parameters, the only option open to them was the business of buying and selling or the profession of accountants. They adopted both and made a grand success of them. Gain and profit became their ultimate calling. It was a foregone conclusion that every Jain child would be adept at counting on his fingertips, and lead a mercantile way of life either as a retailer, wholesaler or a moneylender depending on his station in life. Acquiring wealth thus became

LEFT:
On close observation the ceiling turns out to be a tiered carved compilation of a circular procession of a variety of animals confirming the concern of the Jains for living beings. The dome is made up of eleven concentric rings, five of which are interposed at regular levels and are a record of an ancient half-obliterated memory, handcrafted in pure white marble.

The Dilwara
Complex

LEGEND:

1. Adinatha Vimala Vasahi Temple
2. Neminatha Temple
3. Adinatha Temple
4. Parshvanatha Temple

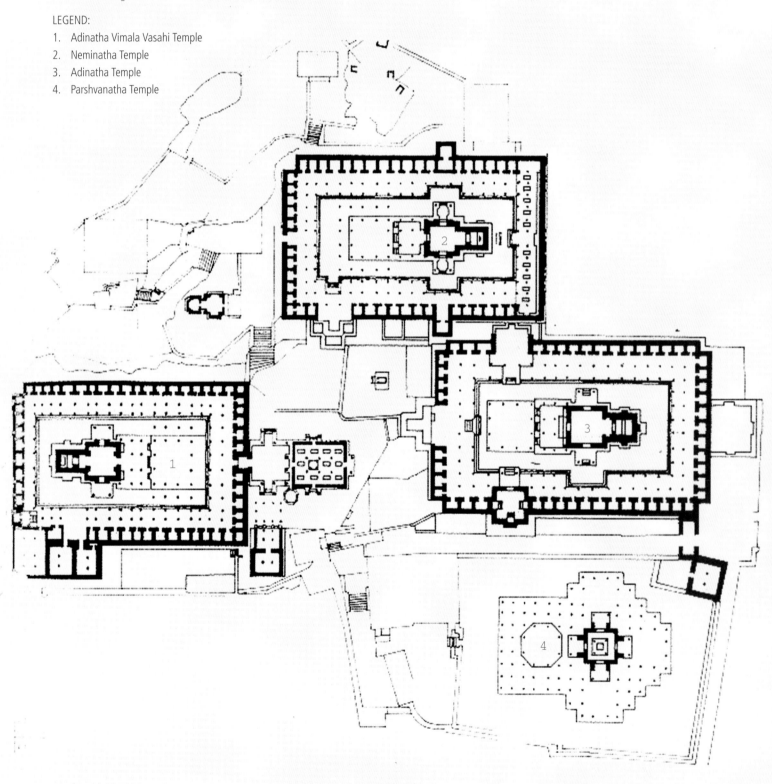

synonymous with the Jains. Some rose to become financiers of kings, who could use the money provided at exorbitant interest rates by the Jains, even to finance wars in which the Jains had their own financial stakes. They pledged their finances to help their ruler win the wars, or they stood to lose even their capital. Surprisingly, they maintained strict frugality in their personal life, constantly fearful as they were of the *Jina* watching over their shoulders, and were wary of indulging in any luxuries.

Riches were accumulated as hard cash, and there were immense reservoirs of money available for the building of temples. In those times money spent on holy acts was exempt from any kind of social censure or imperial taxes. Many of the temple cities became architectural extravaganzas in pristine white marble. Even the lanes, the streets and avenues of the sacred Jain precincts were paved with marble and temples, large and small, lined all of them. The overall scene in the bright afternoon summer sun is dazzling enough to blind the eyes of viewers.

On top of Mount Abu in western Rajasthan just such a city was created. Here, the temple of Dilwara stands out in its magnificence. In its finery and embellishment, it is the most sumptuous of all Jain temples in India. The entrance of the temple is through a domed porch leading to a mandapam that is adorned with a statutory eulogy to the Vimala family, the donors of the temple. Each

Adinatha Vimala Vasahi Temple

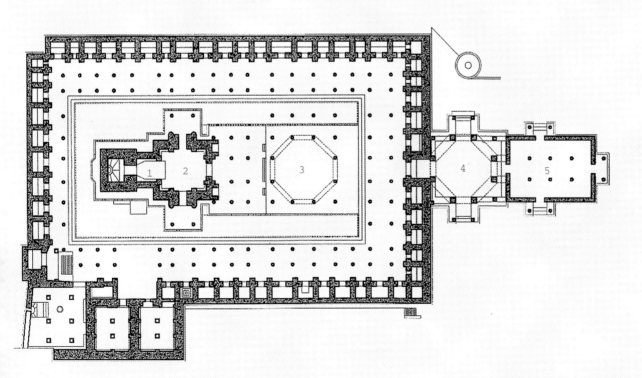

LEGEND:
1. Statue of Mahavira
2. Mandapam
3. Samosan
4. Entrance Hall
5. Vimala Shah Family Gallery
6. Cloisters

Detail of a *Vidyadevi* from
the series of *toranas*
supported by female
figures acting as braces
supporting the vault.

member of the family is sculpted as riding an elephant, and this earthly portrait
gallery is set apart from the shrine of Mahavira.

Octagonally placed at the heart of the *gudha mandapam*, as classified in Jain
terminology, are eight ornamental carved pillars tied to each other by convoluted
but structurally superfluous and profusely decorated brackets. A series of *toranas*
supported by female figures representing *Vidyadevis* acted as braces supporting
the vault. There does not seem to be any need even for the columns since the

ceiling resembles a finely meshed network of a milk-white dream suspended in air as if carrying no weight.

On close observation, the ceiling turns out to be a tiered carved compilation of a circular procession of a variety of animals confirming the concern of the Jains for living beings. The dome is built up of eleven concentric rings, five of which are interposed at regular intervals and are a record of an ancient half-obliterated memory. The six lower ones contain a procession of as many as one hundred and fifty elephants in close rank, depicted from the forefront with intertwined trunks. Above a few mouldings is another border representing images in niches of dancing figures and higher up in the concavity, by images of horsemen. It culminates at the apex with figures engaged in an endless dance leading up to a group of pendent-like festoons of foliage made of transparent white marble seemingly suspended from a high tree in a forest. The ground axis of the entrance culminates in a stern looking statue of Mahavira in an open cell at the end of it. In the entire ductile scheme, the main theme was the multiplicity of the detail, the reiteration of a motif, a ceaseless repetition of images of human form in the belief that the more frequently these are reproduced, the more emphatic is the message they convey.

The impression of passive psychosis is enhanced in the Dilwara Temple by two contradictory aspects—one finicky in its material detail, and the other superhuman. The coldness of the Dilwara Temple at Mount Abu hits the visitor with a blazing fury. The whole temple is unalloyed, uncompromising, pure white marble—floors, columns, traceried ceiling walls and sculptures. All this splendour makes one wonder at the amount of wealth it must have taken to make Dilwara possible although money and finance do not immediately come to mind. However, it is precisely the unlimited use of wealth in a religious cause that is at the core of all Jain architecture in India. It is this dichotomy of personal austerity and religious extravaganza that makes Dilwara such an interesting puzzle.

Generations of masons must surely have gone blind in the white heat of their dedication to the building of the temple. They probably were goaded on by the piercing blood red eyes of the image of the *Jina*, a ruby encrusted as its pupil. A delicate tribute to such a stern *Jina* led to a marriage of opposites and created a friction of its own kind, a friction between austerity and opulence. There is no attempt to paper it over or any attempt to apply a soothing balm. When one leaves the temple, the blaze of the hot sun seems gentle compared to the heated dedication witnessed inside.

Into the Light of Darkness

Meenakshi Temple

Madurai was not built overnight, but over hundreds of years by the three warring dynasties of the south, the Pandayas, the Cholas and the Nayaks. A throbbing, vibrant city of the gods, which houses within its folds the famous Meenakshi Temple, it remained sacred to every dynasty that ruled over it in the past.

Just as a small rural settlement gradually grows into a town over which a city is grafted, the Meenakshi Temple was a village shrine that grew over the years into a holy town to finally become a vibrant metropolis of the gods. To reach even the periphery of this metropolis, visitors have to jostle their way through a maze of suburban lanes and streets that surround the temple.

The journey to the temple is nothing short of an assault on the human senses—the pungent smells of the city include the stinging smell of spices and condiments relieved by wafts of brewing coffee and then dulled by the all pervading odour of cooking fat. A heady mix for delicate nostrils, but if the best way to savour a place is to sniff it then Madurai, with its heady cocktail of aromas, offers a wide selection. The ears are similarly pounded by a cacophony of noises—wailing beggars, the clip-clop of horse-drawn tongas, the strident bells of cycles and rickshaws, the honk of locomotive horns and the roar of buses— all these competing for attention against a background of constant chatter. Add to all this blaring cinema music accompanied by the grating static of loudspeakers and vendors vociferously advertising all kinds of religious trivia and you may get a picture of Madurai. Huge cinema posters adorned with larger-than-life cutouts of heroes and heroines do nothing much for the vision either. It is a bizarre mix of sounds, smells and visuals. Yet, rising majestically above this are the twelve *gopurams*, or pyramidal towers of the temple that preside serenely over the landscape.

On reaching the gateway of the first in the skyline of *gopurams*, the smell changes to the fragrance from the stalls of flower sellers, joss sticks and incense. Down this street, worshippers buy flower garlands, coconuts, bananas and incense sticks—ingredients essential for the rituals of worship. Passing under the second of the many *gopurams*, a large water tank comes into view, the *swarnapushp kandini*, or the tank of the golden lilies. The golden lilies are missing but there are lots of people bathing, clanking their vessels, and chatting around the huge water tank with ghats on all sides, very much like the Indus Valley people may have done in the great bathing tank in Mohenjodaro some five

FACING PAGE:
View of the imposing carved and painted *gopuram*, from inside the complex. Seen beside it is a small mandapam. Many such *gopurams* line the route to the shrine, painted tier upon tier in rich colour.

RIGHT:
The famous 'Hall of
Thousand Pillars' that
measures 240 feet by
250 feet—73 metres
by 76 metres. The hall
took seven years to
build.

thousand years ago. After a purifying dip in the holy tank, the worshipper wraps himself in a *lungi*, adorns his forehead with a white and saffron tilak, and is ready to enter the temple.

Carried along by the buffeting crowd towards the third *gopuram,* the throb of the city at last seems to abate. A medley of sounds from cymbals, drums, gongs and the bells of the shrines are heard. Passing through a tunnel of painted walls and statues of gods and goddesses, the religious part of the journey has at last begun and the next gateway or *gopuram* of the adjacent shrine comes into view.

There are many such *gopurams* along the route to the shrine. Gods, demons, goblins and minor and major ferocious devils teem along the oblong pyramidal surfaces in tier upon tier painted in rich colour. The circumambulatory spaces between successive *gopurams* are filled with the day-to-day activities of their inhabitants. Carvers from a woodcarving workshop are busy around a wooden rath, there is a factory of stonecutters and even a theatre for dance, drama and music. These are regularly interspersed by residences for the temple staff who, work in the administration, maintenance, and accounts offices of the shrine. Naked children roll, play and shout on the thick white blistering sand. Lines of worshippers walk past ringing gongs, clashing cymbals, muttering, singing, chanting and talking.

The temple is a city by itself and provides abundantly for every human need within its own precinct—for living, for celebrating festivals, for prayer and meditation, for shopping, and many other activities. At one time there was a quarter for the *devadasis* too. Originally, they may well have been a venerated group of girls trained in the art of classical dance. With the passing of time and degradation of traditions, they were reduced to becoming prostitutes, practising the age-old profession under a religious umbrella and enriching the coffers of the temple.

Past the many vistas that the temple city offers lies the large, orderly, pillared hall of the mandapam. At last the doors of the goddess, the sanctum sanctorum of Meenakshi, the fish-eyed goddess, is within reach. The entrance to the dark sanctum sanctorum is over a high threshold. After the long and arduous journey the space seems filled with a welcome peace. As the eyes get accustomed to the darkness, the image of the goddess becomes visible, illumined by the lamps of the pujari. There a feeling of an unearthly vibration emitted by some invisible nucleus and a strange intoxicating sensation that one is in the presence of some heavenly apparition. The mind transcends the body and is enthralled by an exquisite experience. However, after a few blessed moments of quiet and peace, the cymbals of the attendant priest break into the calm as they announce the end of the *darshan* of the goddess.

Outside the mood has changed, time has passed and there has been a shift in many scenes in the courtyards. The carpenters have settled down to their midday meal, the stonecutters' factory is silent, and the naked, gambolling children have vanished into the dark shades of the surrounding halls and colonnades. Theatre and dance artists are donning make-up for the evening's performance. The familiar bathing tank appears once again at the near end of the journey through the maze of the temple.

Along the linear journey to the *garbh griha,* are many halls—one larger than the other. The largest needed 985 pillars to support its roof, measuring 240 feet x 250 feet (73 metres x 76 metres). This is the famous 'hall of thousand pillars' that took seven years to build. Another, even larger, was the 350 feet (100.5 metres) deep *choultry* built by Tirumalai Nayak, outside the main precinct of the temple, south of the outermost *gopuram* for the presiding deity of the place, Sundareswar. The hall is 333 feet long and 105 feet broad. It has four rows of pillars supporting a flat roof, and on either side of the central corridor are five architectonic pillars representing ten life-size Nayak rulers in cameos, showing them hunting a wild boar. A second stone corridor follows, with rows of pillars on either side where elephants were kept. The size of the flat roofed halls, commissioned by Vinayak Mudali, a minister of the Nayak kings, necessitated the setting up of an elaborate stonecutters' factory. Column upon column and beam upon beam of a standard design were unendingly churned out of this factory.

How did such an amazing accretion as the Meenakshi Temple come about? It is a long story stretching back over the centuries. Once there were two village shrines, one to Shiva, known here as Sundereswar, and the other to his consort,

RIGHT:
The *swarnapushp kandini*, or the tank of the golden lilies, with ghats on all sides, very much like the Indus Valley bathing tank of Mohenjadaro.

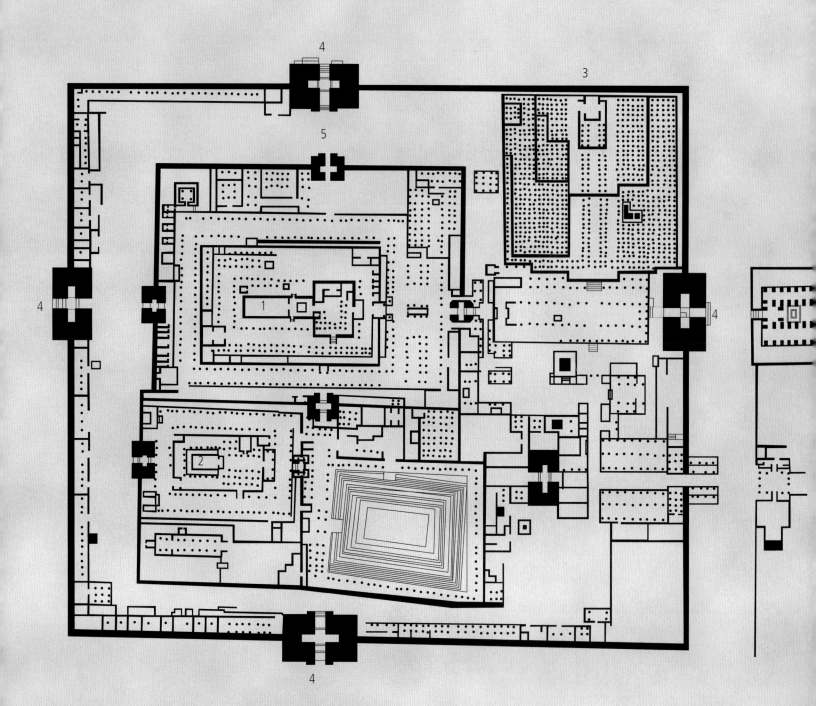

Meenakshi Temple Complex

LEGEND:
1. Shrine
2. Sundereswar Shrine
3. Hall of 1000 Pillars
4. Gopuram
5. Parikrama
6. Tirumalai Nayak
   Choultry

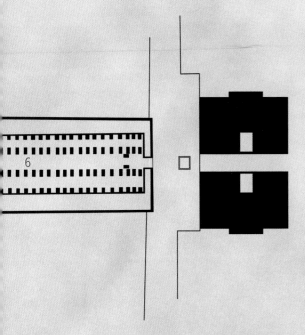

Meenakshi. The epic story is told of how goddess Meenakshi, who at one time was deformed because she had three breasts, acquired Sundereswar as her consort and shed one of her breasts. These individual shrines for the divine couple are the focal point of a hugely popular fertility cult centred on the coupling god and goddess, that is supposed to maintain the preservation and regeneration of the universe.

As each shrine expanded it intruded upon the space of the adjacent ones. Finally, a merger took place and a large wall encompassing both the temples was built. The overall plan may appear a jumble, but when studied, a logical plan emerges. It is seen that there are concentric walls with *gopurams* in the north, east and south of each circumambulation. It is the skyline of the temple that goes from symmetry to the unsymmetrical. Over a period of time with the accretion of greater religious merit and with pilgrims arriving in thousands to attend religious festivities stretching over days, the temple precinct needed to be enlarged further. The methodology of growth had by now been established, and more space was acquired, defined by yet another larger concentric wall. *Gopurams* adorned the walls and rose skyward to form a graceful skyline, attracting more and more pilgrims to the modest but ancient shrines within.

The last concentric boundary wall around the main shrines had the distinct feel of a blank fortified wall. Looming somewhere in the background of the builders' and rulers' mind was the threat of the Muslim invaders that had already devastated the outermost defences of south India. The temples were beginning to acquire the characteristics of a fortress, behind which the population could seek refuge in the event of an attack. Fortunately for the kingdom, it never came to that. The Muslims did not reach so far down south, but the temple city was large enough to accommodate the populace and temporarily hold out behind the walls of the holy temple at the centre of the city of Madurai.

Vijayanagar Divine City

In the valley of the Tungabhadra River, and sprawled over on the surrounding ridges, hidden in crevasses or perched atop huge rocks, are the amazing ruins of the ancient city of Vijayanagar. The boulders of the neighbouring barren hills stand like natural monolithic sentries of the city clad in a variety of colours ranging from gray and brown to pink.

The birth and death of the city was enacted against the dramatic conflicting background of a rugged boulder-strewn landscape and the calm peaceful valley of the Tungabhadra. The river flows twisting and turning between the ridges, rushing over boulders as it winds its way northeast to broaden momentarily into a wide basin. On its banks on either side is laid out the city centre of Vijayanagar, the celebrated 'City of Victory.' A victory not won in war, but through court intrigue, a victory celebrated by building a new city in a God-given landscape.

The ridges surrounding the valley are marked with the remains of the many gateways that once punctuated the concentric walls and stand today as the isolated sentinels of the sprawling city. Within the walls of the citadel and at the heart of Vijayanagar there are the plinths of buildings that are obvious remains of royal palaces. So beautiful are these coursed and moulded terraces that if their superstructures matched them in any way, they justify the eulogies of countless visitors to the city in its heyday. The Persian ambassador Abdu'r Razzaq records: 'The city of Bidjanagar is such that the pupil of the eye has never seen a place like it and the ear of intelligence has never been informed that there existed anything to equal it in the world. It is built in such a manner that seven citadels and the same number of concentric walls enclose each other.'

The royal infrastructure of Vijayanagar was destroyed by a confederation of Islamic armies that won a decisive war against the armies of Krishnadevraya's son at Talikota in 1565. A vicious devastation followed. 'Never perhaps in the history of the world had such havoc been wrought on so splendid a city. The magnificent stone carvings were smashed to pieces with crow bars and hammers and where it defied human efforts, fires were lit to burst it open,' writes a chronicler of the times.

The series of low ridges that surround the ruins act as a natural cantonment for the city. They slope gradually down to the valley and are sparsely forested. Through the thin woods one can discern the fractured remnants of fort walls, running over boulders and bridging deep crevasses to delineate the boundaries of the settlement. The environs of Vijayanagar are like a planetary cyclorama—a

tumbled jungle of blasted boulders that seem to have been scattered over the surrounding ridges either by a geological upheaval or by some unearthly power.

The secular and strategic functions of the city may have vanished in the carnage but the more enthralling works of architecture nestled in the protective folds of nature have survived the ravages of war and time. The architecture is deeply embedded into the landscape and in time the natural rock itself became the foundations of an imposing superstructure with the cliffs of the hills guarding it zealously against calamities. It is indeed difficult to say where nature ends and art begins for it is an ever binding fusion of nature with architecture. Simple shrines are intimately blended into the earth, some carved out of caverns and fissures, others perched on hills of stone. Some temples even enclose ancient rock grottoes within their finely designed exteriors. Many such temples and architectural curios are scattered all over the countryside, some within and others outside the city, some urban and others suburban.

Wonderful stone temples survive amidst the desolate countryside. In the southwest of city is the Raghunatha Temple on the Malyavanta Hill, the principal shrine of which is built around a natural boulder, on which images of gods have

LEFT:
The Tungabhadra River flows twisting and turning warily between the ridges, rushing over boulders as it winds its way northeast to broaden momentarily into a wide basin. On its banks on either side is laid out the city centre of Vijayanagar, the celebrated 'City of Victory.'

ABOVE:
A Chariot of God
mounted on a
platform with wheels
so engineered that at
one time they could
be revolved by hand.

FACING:
Ground plan of the
Vijayanagar complex.

been carved. This shrine is at the centre of an enclosure of columned halls and sub-shrines. On a rock plateau of the same hill, overlooking the river, is the Krishna Temple, which consists of a large open courtyard containing the principal shrine, which is a natural boulder carved with the images of Rama and Sita. Elsewhere, there are innumerable small shrines built like architectural grottos, sunk into the craggy landscape. The Hazari Ram, commissioned as a private chapel, has a hundred-columned hall, each of which is elaborately sculptured. In the western zone of the city is the Virupaksha Temple, the shrine of which is enclosed in a ring of concentric rectangular walls with a columned hall erected on the southern side outside. The hall is almost choked inside not by mere columns but with huge architectonic piers. Any concept of space is devoured by clusters of such piers that highlight the skills of the sculptors. Architecture has a secondary role to play in these creations.

The Vithalla Temple dominates a group of temples further down the river. In the centre of its courtyard is a Chariot of God mounted on a platform with wheels so engineered that at one time they could be revolved by hand. The temple is spread over a large area within which are shrines and columned halls and kitchens for preparing food for feasts, all enclosed by a rectangular colonnade. Each column in the colonnade is fashioned out of a single block of granite, and interposed between their shafts is a half natural, half mythical relief of a rearing lion, resurrected like a ghost from an ancient past. It was not really great architecture, but a celebration of the massive, in the round sculpted piers, columns and shafts. Within the *Kalyan* Mandapam of the temple, which has

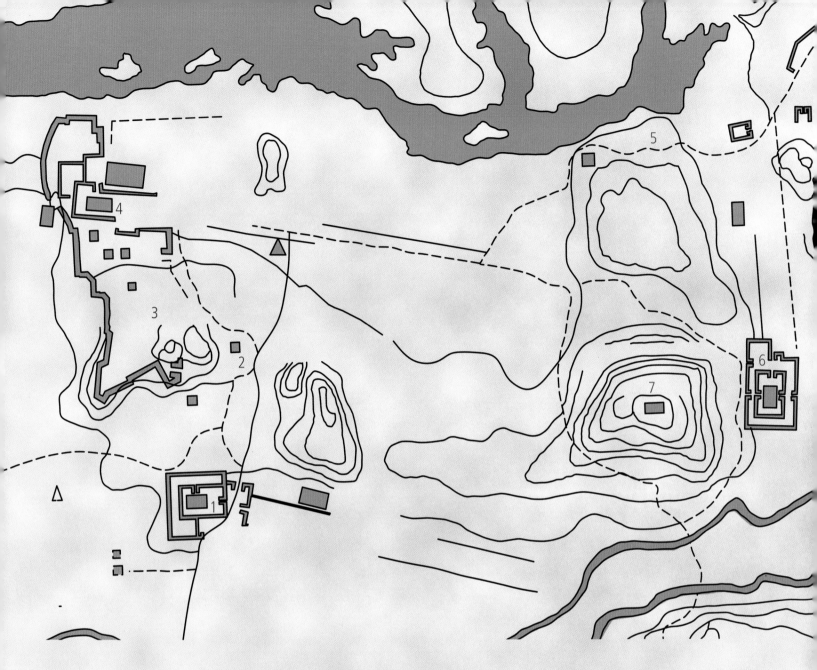

twelve pillars around a square throne in the centre of the hall, weddings of gods and goddesses were celebrated annually. The Kondandarama Temple on the banks of the Tungabhadra beneath Matanga Hill marks the coronation site of a royal divinity. All these temples are florid works of creativity and religious intensity and have remained centres of pilgrimage through the centuries, proving to be more lasting than the temporal culture of the court.

The site for divine weddings, the ubiquitous throne and the coronation venue within the site of the temples were subtle reminders to the worshippers of the powers that permitted the king to rule as a defender of Hindu faith and protector of its sacred images. The equation of terrestrial and celestial worlds meant that the king exercised the heroic and legendary qualities of his divine counterpart. He assumed that his royal city was inhabited by a perfect Hindu society, protected by the royal shield of power bestowed by divine right. This fluid boundary between the divine and royal realms is an assertive peculiarity of

LEGEND:
1. Krishna Temple
2. Monolithic Ganesha
3. Hemakta Hill
4. Virupaksha Temple
5. Kondandarama Temple
6. Venkateshwara Temple
7.   Matanga Hill

Vijayanagar. Just as the gap between architecture and nature was bridged, so also was that between royalty and divinity, an ideal Hindu capital was the city of both kings and gods. The more the kings aggrandized themselves the more they were perceived to be the warriors of the gods. Royalty had indeed worked out a very convenient arrangement with divinity; the city that they built was to the glory of the gods, which reflected equally on to their own regal selves.

It can be determined by conjecture that the royal or temporal city centre of Vijayanagar was formally approached through a series of axially placed *gopurams*. In view, however, of the irregularity of the ground on which the centre was built, total symmetry in its town planning was not envisioned and the disposition of the different quarters of the city cannot be easily determined. But what can be seen is that within one portion of the walled area were grouped the imperial buildings, while the second, more public space stands south, in the middle of the water basin of the Tungabhadra and reached by a bridge.

Today, one can barely discern the thirty-four streets that existed before the military holocaust. 'Each of these streets was as wide as tourneys, selling all sorts of precious stones, cloth, horses, and every sort of things on earth,' writes the

ABOVE:
The imposing Vithalla statue at Vijayanagar.

RIGHT:
Ground plan and elevation of the Balakrishna Temple.

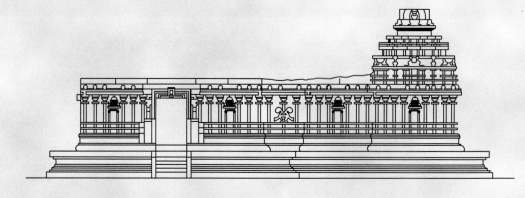

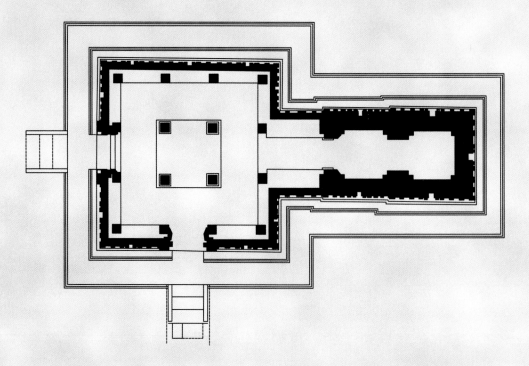

Portuguese traveller Pae in his memoirs. 'To service this city two thousand beasts of burden entered the city everyday with all kinds of merchandise.... The markets are always overflowing with an abundance of fruits, grapes, oranges, limes, pomegranate, jackfruit and mangoes, and all very cheap.' To service the city there were many intra-structural buildings in an enclosed citadel in the shallow valley. These included circular masonry granaries and pavilions with internal water basins, tanks and wells, which ensured a regular supply of water for the city.

The remains of open columned pavilions, colonnades, and enclosed houses, whose ruins now flank the main 'street', were lodgings for pilgrims, rest-houses for royal visitors and shops for merchants. Also included among the houses and shops were the quarters of the euphemistic handmaidens of god offering their own variety of blandishments in what was the market of love and one of the joyous sights of the capital. 'The splendour of the houses of the handmaidens and the beauty of the heart ravishers and their sensuous ogles were temptation enough. The king was tempted and the maids attended to the monarch during his time of relaxation. Otherwise, they participated as dancing girls along with the musicians, wrestlers and parade of troops on horses and elephants at the sacrifices of animals.' It must have been indeed a City of Joy at the zenith of its prosperity.

It was too good to last of course. Everything caved in: the architecture reduced itself to endless colonnaded halls and corridors. The sculptors began to create images of women wantonly displaying their bodies. It was obvious that the kings and their overriding ambition and greed had virtually destroyed the garb of divinity and corrupted its citizens as well as the holy clergy. The end of the city was imminent and ultimately it came in the form of a cataclysmic war. And a morally sapped city was destroyed. The end of this City of Victory was as ignoble as its birth was noble. It was deserted forever thereafter. And with its death came the end of Hindu revivalism.

Qutub Minar

Ascent of the Crescent

Tall structures have held a strange fascination for all who see them and through the ages, they have challenged man's creativity and captivated his imagination. The credit for building the tallest structure in the world today is hotly contested amongst architects and builders, and many records have been made and broken. In the last century, the Empire State Building in New York held the record for a very long period followed by the Chicago Tower, the former World Trade Center Towers in New York and now the Petronas Towers in Malaysia.

The same spirit of competition went into the building of tall structures in historic times: the pyramids, victory and commemorative towers—leaning and otherwise—the *minars,* spires of Islamic architectural style, the *stambhas,* the ziggurats and temple and church spires, all reached for the sky and were assertions of confidence and the primacy of individual faiths.

With the advent of Islam in India, the *minar* became a common feature of the new building style brought by the Muslims. Islamic theology extols the *minar* or *Qutub,* as a pole and axis and the pivot of Justice, Sovereignty, and of the Faith that casts the shadow of God from the west to the east. Yusuf I, by raising the Giralda at Seville in Spain, and Iltutmish by completing the Qutub at Delhi at about the same time, ensured that the shadow of Allah fell over the entire Islamic world of the thirteenth century, stretching from Spain to India.

The famous Qutub Minar of Delhi was begun in A.D. 1199. The height of the tower, as it stands today, is 72.5 metres (238 feet). Many subsequent *minars* were built in India but none exceeded its height. There was the Char Minar at Daulatabad, the Feroze Minar at Gaur, the Chor Minar at Fatehpur Sikri, and hundreds of others attached to mosques and tombs. The only one that could have challenged it was proposed in its immediate vicinity. It threatened to be taller than the Qutub because its diameter at the base was larger. But unfortunately after its foundations were laid and only a rubble stump completed, it was abandoned due to the political conditions of the time. Had it been completed the view of a pair of neighbouring monumental skyscrapers standing together would have been a glorious sight.

What is amazing is that the Muslims dared to build the Qutub when they were still struggling to stabilize the sovereignty of Islam over India. But the man who conceived it had planned the Qutub as a morale-boosting symbol of supremacy and an architectural emblem of politics and power.

RIGHT:
The Qutub, by its
imposing height, was a
morale-boosting symbol
of supremacy and an
architectural emblem of
politics and power.

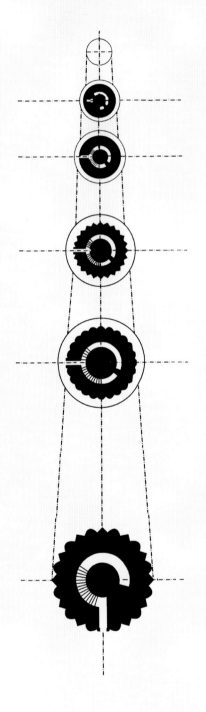

Mohammed of Ghori, a Turkoman slave, and the leader of a confederation of Turkish and Afghan soldiers had vanquished the disorganized Hindu armies in the battlefield of Tarain. The Muslim armies had earlier been defeated here by those of Prithiviraj Chauhan, the Rajput ruler of Delhi and Ajmer, but they were undeterred and challenged him yet again at the same battlefield. The Muslim armies must have 'spent the night before the battle telling their beads, and the Hindu soldiers listening to the stories of heroes recited by their bards.' The battle that ensued between the two titans spearheading different faiths was fierce and politically as consequential as the fabled war of the Mahabharata because it changed the entire social and political history of India thereafter. On that historic blood-drenched field neither legendary Rajput valour nor ponderous elephants could prevail upon the mounted mobile archers of the Muslims. Like a great building, the Hindu house tottered and collapsed in its own ruins that literally became the foundations of a refreshing architectural movement that pumped fresh blood into the exhausted and languishing building arts of India.

Ghori, who had invaded India to plunder and loot, left behind Qutub-ud-din Aibak, another slave-general in his army, as governor and perfunctorily commissioned him to consolidate Islamic power in India. Mohammed died soon after leaving India, and the governor immediately declared independence from the authority of the Ghoris, who were preoccupied elsewhere. Qutub-ud-din was left as the only recognized Muslim ruler in India, and his immediate religious obligation was to build a mosque in an Islamic encampment in conquered territory. However, to build the mosque virtually overnight, as ordained by his faith, was a daunting task indeed—the Muslim armies had been accompanied by military engineers to help them win wars, but not to build monuments to celebrate the glory of Islam.

The rulers had perforce to recruit Indian master builders who had proven skills. They belonged to an ancient guild of professional craftsmen willing to work for any worthy patron or ruler, and had interpreted different faiths into architectural forms, and duly fulfilled their contractual obligations. They did not let religion or faith come in the way of their skills and economic survival. Qutub-ud-din astutely decided to employ the members of the guild to engineer all his structures guided by Islamic architectural aspirations. In other words, the engineers and craftsmen of the guild would physically realize the desired elevations construed by the rulers. No verbal communication was possible between the two, but then visual language transcends the verbal, and artistic commonalities are more easily shared. The Hindus grasped what the Muslims wanted and demonstrated their capability in achieving the desired shapes of arches and domes but by their own structural methods.

Given time, this arrangement could work. Stone was mined from the quarries and cut, trenches had to be dug for the foundations and plinths erected for the superstructure to commence. But time was not at hand. The king was busy fighting battles to consolidate the fluid boundaries of his territory. The faithful had to have their masjid, literally, a place of prostration, and the king, a monument to impress upon the subjugated 'infidels' the power of the rituals of Islam.

If mining stone from quarries, digging trenches and laying foundations was a cumbersome task, was there a quicker alternative? To the strategic military mind of Qutub-ud-din, a Ghazi, a holy soldier of Islam, the solution was staring him in the face. It was the twenty-seven-odd Hindu and Jain temples of the capital city of Prithviraj. These were constructed with dry stone masonry and could be pulled down and ready-made stones, columns, beams and roofing units retrieved intact from them. A new building could be erected with them as easily as a child builds from a set of blocks.

It was a brilliant idea indeed, a double-edged sword that would send an appropriate message to both the conquered and the victorious. The destruction of the temples would be a crushing blow to the already flagging spirit of the erstwhile rulers and would satisfy the iconoclastic zeal of the Sunni Muslims who had overcome them. It would also impress upon the people of India, that Islam had arrived to stay, build, and rule and not merely to raid, loot and vanish.

The process of construction started immediately with the copious supply of building blocks obtained from the dismantled temples. The east-west axis of a Hindu temple fortunately coincided with that of the mosque whose rear had to face Mecca, that lay west of India. This enabled the builders to immediately begin building the superstructures over the ready-made substructure. The material recovered from the temples was erected over the plinths of the outer walls transforming it into a colonnade surrounding the rectangular courtyard of the mosque. The deep *liwan* on the west was composed of three parallel colonnades, covered by pyramidal roofing units uprooted from the demolished temples. The carven images of gods on the columns were deliberately disfigured and hidden under thick plaster as were the pyramidal roof units sheathed with rubble and mortared over to resemble shallow domes. The essentials of the Quwwat-ul-Islam, Power of Islam, mosque of Delhi were thus hurriedly assembled together.

The mosque was erected symmetrically around an ancient Ashokan Pillar of iron that was apparently built in celebration of Buddhism, but due to its piquant ancestry, both Hindus and Muslims alike respected it. The purity of its iron on which no rust has ever accumulated over the ages is a mystery till today.

ABOVE:
Details of the flanges showing calligraphy works and decorations typical of Islamic architecture.

FACING PAGE:
Inner elevation plan of the Qutub.

The fundamental elements of a mosque had been achieved, and the religious obligation of the ruler duly met. However, something seemed amiss. The mosque did not quite look like those that the Muslim migrants were used to seeing at home. The *liwan* was a pedestrian assembly of plastered Hindu columns and looked like a *jhopra* in stone. The familiar skyline of large domes, long spanned arches and tall minarets was missing. Qutub-ud-din set about remedying this and ordered the construction of a stone screen of large arches in front of the *liwan*. To fulfil this command, a more intimate amalgamation of Islamic intentions and Hindu workmanship was inevitable. The Hindu builders would shape the large arches of the screen from trabeate corbelling and cut the corners of projecting stones to shape smooth arches for the stone screen. The arches were framed with Muslim inscriptions, copied blindly by the Hindu builders from samples provided by the Muslims. The mosque now seemed more 'Islamic'. Yet, something was still grossly amiss. It was the *Qutub*, the pivotal axis of Islam.

Qutub-ud-din decided to build a tall tower within the mosque precincts in the southeast corner that would be visible from the wide plains surrounding this encampment in the Aravalli Hills of Delhi. How to build it was left to the Islamic army engineers turned architects, and the recognized skill of the Hindu builders.

The foundation and its depth was laid in proportion to the projected height of the *minar*. Encased within the fifteen-metres wide rubble masonry of the outer walls of the minarets was a staircase. The masonry from the plinth upwards inclined inwards to maintain a stable centre of gravity for the entire shaft that gradually slackened to the first balcony. For the projection to hold up the gallery there was a system of oversailing corbelled arches protruding outwards from the *minar*. The rubble masonry of the outer surface of the shaft was shaped into alternate triangular and semicircular flanges, which were panelled in red sandstone.

The *minar* was built up to the second storey by Qutub-ud-din, and was completed by Iltutmish his accomplished successor. Seeing great virtue in the structure, Iltutmish delegated his architect, Amir Koh, to build the tower higher. Amir Koh continued building only the angular flanges of the masonry due to the diminishing diameter of the *minar*, and built it up to an unknown intended height of the incomplete *minar*. An earthquake is said to have brought down some storeys, which were later completed with an encasing of marble either by him or his successors. However, the building of the Qutub Minar had raised the status of Delhi as it flagged the axiom that 'He who rules Delhi, rules India'.

By now, the Hindu builders had grasped the arcuate system of Muslim building and for the Khaljis, the successors of the so-called Slave Dynasty, they built the Alai Darwaza with true arches of modest proportions. The pioneering attempt to use a new structural technique may have seemed trifling, but it was a pathfinder to the greater building achievements of the Muslims. The *Darwaza* was panelled with a blend of red sandstone and white marble. The Indian carver diligently stencilled in the Quranic inscriptions bordering the flanges. The jambs of the arched openings are adorned with pairs of slender pilasters, resembling Hindu temple columns, and the intrados of the arch ornamented with the so-called 'spear head fringe', devised by the stone carvers. The *Alai Darwaza* designed as an entrance hall with a gate, to the existing mosque complex proved to be the module of all the architectural endeavours of the Muslim. The cube of the gateway symmetrically punctuated by true arches duly domed over was the kernel of future Islamic building activities in India. All Islamic buildings were an assembly of such modules in varying sizes and patterns; it was the alphabet of the Islamic language of building.

With the completion of the *Alai Darwaza* the Khaljis had become powerful enough to build their own city of Jahan Panah in the neighbourhood of the Qutub. Their successors shifted their capital to the fortress of Tughlaqabad. The days of the glory of the earliest Muslim encampment in the country were on the wane though the permanent settlement that exists around it has survived till today. The new Islamic building sites are indeed engaging, but the earliest footprints of Islam in India are indelible, and the Qutub Minar is an omnipresent and tall reminder of the glorious courage of the pioneers of Islamic rule in India.

BELOW:
Isometric elevation of the Qutub Complex.

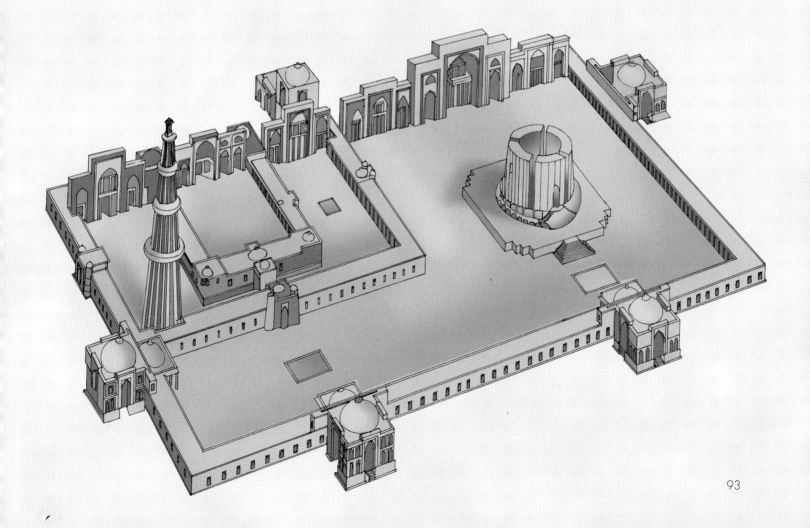

Fatehpur Sikri

Grand Red Folly

In 1556 Humayun, the son of the founder of the Mughal Dynasty, Babur, met a sudden and tragic end when he slipped down the staircase of his library and plunged to his death. His son Akbar succeeded him, inheriting the Mughal throne when he was only a mere boy of thirteen. Completely unlettered and incapable of writing and reading when he ascended the throne, Akbar enjoyed and encouraged all the arts, listened to the recitation of the finest poetry for hours, and what is most relevant, loved gardens and fine buildings. This young boy was to grow into the greatest Mughal and among the finest rulers of the country.

The great Mughal was at his whimsical best when he decided to build the palace-city of Fatehpur Sikri. This outstanding work of architecture is evidence of the fact that Akbar was, innately a constructive man with a humanitarian vision—a term, which, by its very nature encompasses all points of view. After all, he himself was the child of a Sunni father, a Shia mother, born in Hindustan, on the soil of Sufism, in the house of a Hindu.

In 1569, he decided that he had had enough of the intrigues of royalty, the courtiers, and the corruption they had bred among the people of his capital city of Agra. Even though he had invested much time and wealth in building a massive fort in Agra, he was now determined to shift his capital city elsewhere. The royal gaze turned towards Sikri.

Why he chose Sikri is a question that has befuddled many: one of the reasons may be that Akbar in his quest for the birth of an heir had visited many Sufi saints. On one such pilgrimage, he visited a saint who lived on a red sandstone hillock called Sikri, about forty kilometres from Agra. Sheikh Salim Chisti, blessed him with a child, and luckily for both the emperor and the saint, the prayers and wishes of both were granted. When it was ascertained that Jodha Bai, Akbar's wife, was with child the Mughal emperor sent her to live in the saint's hermitage on the hill, where she gave birth to their son, Salim. In gratitude to Sheikh Chisti and to suit his own strategic aims, Akbar, true to his character, made a swift decision. Without wasting time on mandatory bureaucratic and technical reports on the project, he declared the Sikri Hill as the site of his new capital city.

Earlier, the long ridge-like hill had been sparsely inhabited by Sufi saints and the Sikriwal Rajputs, who had settled here after a combined force of Rajput kings had lost a decisive battle to Babur, on the plains immediately below. In fact, it was this battle that had opened the floodgates for Mughal domination in India.

FACING PAGE:
The imposing and grand *Buland Darwaza* is the main entrance through which the Fatehpur Sikri complex is entered. It was added to the southern side of the Jama Masjid in Fatehpur Sikri to celebrate Akbar's many martial victories.

Ground Plan of Fatehpur Sikri

LEGEND:

1 Court Of Public Audience
2 Turkish Sultana's Garden
3 Pachisi Court
4 Girl's School
5 Turkish Sultana's House
6 Turkish Sultana's Bath
7 Sleeping Quarters
8 Char Chaman
9 Court of Private Audience
10 Emperor's Study
11 Hospital
12 Panch Mahal
13 Miriam's House
14 Miriam's Garden
15 Nagina Masjid
16 Birbal's House
17 Stables
18 Jodhabai's Palace
19 Bath
20 Administration and Archives

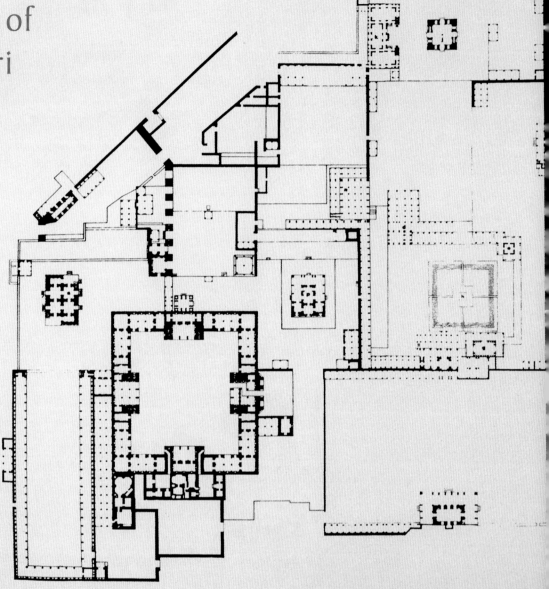

It is also possible that Akbar's decision to build his capital here may have been in commemoration of his grandfather's triumphant victory.

Once the decision was taken, Akbar lost no time in commencing construction of the city. Speed was, in fact, the essence of the spirit of this capital city; speed in need, in conception, in building, in populating it, and, ironically, speed too, in deserting it. Fatehpur Sikri was built on an emperor's whim, but deserted for a reason. Too many courtiers and noblemen, as well as the common populace had begun dying of typhoid and dysentery, because of the contaminated water supply. Earlier technical reports must have cautioned Akbar about the quality of water, which Akbar had either ignored or felt he could remedy, and there must have also been other strategic reasons for doing so. Ultimately, Akbar abandoned the city altogether. Later, some of the minor Mughal kings used it for fun and

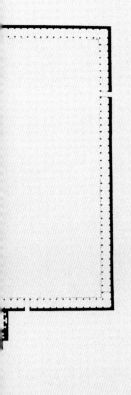

ABOVE:
Elevation of Fatehpur Sikri.

frolic. Surprisingly, most of the buildings of the city have survived virtually intact for posterity. Since the Indian climate is gentle to stone, even today, the visitor is led to believe that Sikri was completed only yesterday.

What exists of the structures today is almost as they must have been over four hundred years ago. The palace centre that came up first appears more a resting point rather than a permanent abode. It seems like an army camp that was established at stage halts for an emperor on the move during a military campaign: a virtual city of 'tents in stone', that could seemingly be shifted overnight. Yet it takes little imagination to people this city with the Mughal aristocracy, to hear soldiers marching over the paved areas, and at night to hear the ladies talk and laugh through screens and trillages of their private domains. Many fanciful stone pavilions for the use of royalty stretches the imagination a bit further and the sound of ladies, bejewelled with jingling anklets, enlivening the giant *chaupat* court where the game was played using the ladies as the *pyaadas*. Screams of mischievous joy can be heard (figuratively speaking) as *aankh mi chauli* was played in a chamber close to the *Diwan-i-Khas*, as the guide will ask you to believe, though it was probably just the secretariat of the royal court.

Each of these 'stone tents' was built by guilds of craftsmen invited from different parts of the empire and given free reign to express the art of their region. But all of them had to execute their skills in the only building material made available to them—the soft red sandstone quarried from the site itself—carve on it, make traceries, *jaalis*, staircases, pilasters or even paint on their surface. It was the shrewd dictates of economics of building that made the emperor enforce this restriction. Somehow the red sandstone endears itself to people visiting it even today, making them feel comfortable and not in awe of their surroundings.

The city palace thus emerged as an ensemble of all the diverse Indian architectural forms of that time, merging together into a meaningful eclectic chiaroscuro, an architectural signal of Akbar's secular political philosophy. Hindu builders from neighbouring Gujarat, Gwalior and Rajasthan were invited to design some buildings at designated places. Skilled rural craftsmen were free to build the familiar sloping roofs of imitation terracotta tiles or blue glazed tiles. Designers set new patterns of building in erecting the *Panch Mahal* and the *Diwan-i-Khas* with ideas that alluded to ancient Indians forms; the Ashokan-type pillar, supported by multiple Jain brackets to hold the emperor's seat in the *Diwan-i-Khas*, the terraces of the *Panch Mahal* alluding to the viharas of the Buddhists, and a complete Jain pavilion known as the 'astrologer's seat' prominently located on the side of the *Daftar Khana*.

All these diverse ideas were held together by an architectural vision, guided by Akbar himself. This vision was exercised with a precise methodology, which runs right through the complex, bringing to the eye a constant change of view. The focus shifts from building to building and all this is achieved by a subtle

architectural master plan. This plan has symmetrical compositions interspersed by an asymmetrical but geometric system of axis, all at right angles with each other. Point-counterpoint of solids and voids of the colonnades and the heavy line of the *chajjas* almost anticipate the spatial rhythms of contemporary (or modernist) work. The *Diwan-i-Khas*, the *Khwabgah* and the Courts of Justice are along a central axis that is the backbone of the *Pachisi Court*. From the intermediary focal points of this axis, shoot out other trajectories which enmesh the entire layout in a measurable right-angle grid that determines the location of all other buildings. The open courtyards in the layout are designed according to a very elementary system of proportions; they are all in whole numbers. It is either 1:1 or 1:2 or 1:3 or 1:4 and so on. The focal points too are also located strictly according to this rule. The unit of measurement thus did not matter; it could have been feet, yards, metres or the *'ilahi-gaz'*, it is the elementary numbers that mattered.

ABOVE:
Aerial view of Fatehpur
Sikri, an architectural
vision guided by Akbar
and executed with
precise methodology
which runs right through
the complex, bringing to
the eye a constant
change of view.

The so-called *Jodha Bai Palace*, named after Akbar's wife, is the only one that defies the grid. The building, once the royal harem, was either the starting point of the whole venture, when the grid system had not been perfected, or the end, and was located to suit Akbar's personal needs. The overall grid, however, encompassed all the other buildings of the palace: the *Diwan-i-Aam*, the *Diwan-i-Khas*, the *Pachisi Court*, the water tank in front of the *Khwabgah*, where great music and dance festivals were held, the many independent mansions for his favourite queens, the stables for the horses, the hospital and many more buildings.

There were courtyards in some buildings connected together by colonnaded passageways—some secret, some only for the use of nobility and some purely for utilitarian purposes. Down the corridors of this ghost town marched soldiers on their daily manoeuvres or passed courtiers in procession preceding the emperor to announce his arrival. Such a palace city has never been built again in India or anywhere else in the world. It is a unique building venture, which only Akbar could have duplicated—but never did.

Standing vigilantly over the fanciful palace of the city is the Jama Masjid complex laid strictly according to Allah's will. The plan of this is totally symmetrical, laid out like a conventional mosque. It has a large courtyard with a deep colonnade protecting the *mehrab* in the west, with three gateways at the cardinal points. It is the largest historical mosque in India and stands at the western end of the palace complex. Its huge courtyard has been embellished with the beautiful white trellised marble *dargah* of Saint Salim Chisti; nearby there are also a few other tombs. The *Buland Darwaza* was added onto the south side of the mosque to celebrate Akbar's many martial victories. It was also added on the demands of the orthodox Muslims who wanted the mosque to be the most prominent building of the capital city, looming taller than all others. From its style it is apparent that the Persian builders of Humayun's tomb were commissioned to design and construct this gate as per the wishes of the clergy.

Below the northern end of the mosque, Akbar built a modest hall for himself and his chosen companions. Here he held religious discourses with the elite of all religions who visited his court. He propounded the concept of a new religious philosophy called *Din-e-Ilahi*, and presented it as an alternative that challenged many of the tenets of Islamic orthodoxy. These attempted inroads into the domains of the clergy met with little success. The time was not yet ripe for the birth of a new religion that challenged the existing orthodoxy of so many others.

Ironically, in one of the stone tablets on the *Buland Darwaza*, the emperor himself had inscribed the words, 'the world is a bridge; cross it but build no houses on it.' The mercurial Akbar realized his folly as rapidly as he had created it and abandoned Sikri with characteristic alacrity, leaving for posterity, a 'city of misadventure' worth visiting many times, because follies on such a gargantuan scale are rarely ever built.

99

BELOW:
Elevation of Fatehpur Sikri.

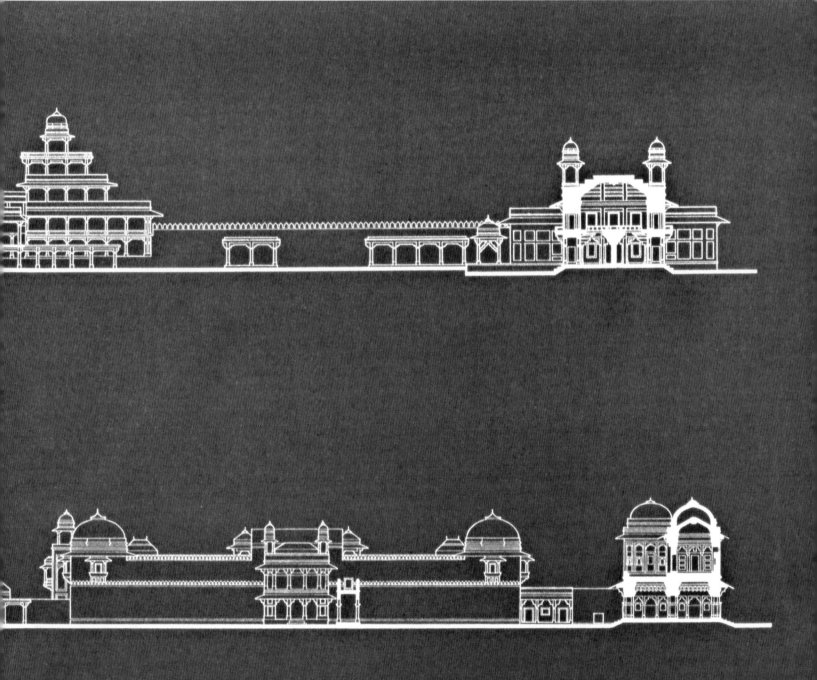

Gol Gumbaz

Bubble Over Bleakness

The largest dome built in the world, the Gol Gumbaz, towers over a very substantial group of splendid architectural monuments. Unfortunately, all of them are situated in the town of Bijapur, which seems undeserving of them. The plan of the city is devoid of any discernible pattern, centre or axis of streets or avenues. It is a haphazard maze of dusty roads roughly girdling the Ark-Qilla Fort, which is enclosed by a wall about a mile long surrounding an area of 1,300 acres. There is no memorable history of its growth and no geographical context to its location; it is not on the banks of a river or below a secure hilltop nor does it have any distinguishing topographical features. It is difficult to believe that this lacklustre city was the capital of an empire that at one time spanned the country from coast to coast.

A significant fact of its history is that it was built on the site of the ancient town of Bichkanhalli that contained Hindu temples. The Muslim conquerors found these shrines in ruins and used the materials from their rubble to construct sundry structures like gateways, guardrooms and the Old Mosque. The mosque had to be built quickly and by religious ordinance because it was incumbent on the ruler to build it immediately in any territory conquered by Islam.

The attraction of the town lies in its architectural monuments that are the heart and soul of the city. Yusuf I, the founder of the Adil Shahi Dynasty (1489–1686), that ruled Bijapur during the entire span of the city's political prominence, had inspired in his successors a structural ardour that resulted in a profuse display of fine buildings in the city. The buildings may look severe and stern from the outside, but they are adorned with splendid huge ogee-shaped arches, large domes and graceful minarets. Constructions used plastered stone, brick masonry and included exquisite timberwork, although, the use of wood is a rarity in Muslim royal structures. Among the innumerable buildings, the more prominent were Ibrahim's mosque axially connected to another mosque; its entirety is referred to as a *rauza*. The *rauza* was decorated in a manner peculiar to Bijapur. Large surfaces were left plainly plastered while clearly demarcated bands and patches in local basalt stone were engraved by local Hindu craftsmen. This contrast between large plain areas and vivid sculptured surfaces is typical of all the buildings of Bijapur, including the prominent *Gagan* and *Angur Mahals* or palaces and the *Mehtar Darwaza*, a gateway. Their grandeur is calculated to captivate the viewer with its own visual sensations, rather than in any way enhance the views of the town.

The royal court of Bijapur, a seemingly brilliant but insular royal institution, was commendably free of any signs of bigotry. It offered its abundant hospitality to many learned men and valiant officers from Persia, Turkestan and Rum, and several eminent artists who prospered under the largesse of the Adil Shahi kings. But the history of the Adil Shahis themselves is one of endless violence and the royal palaces within the citadel were frequently dyed with blood during royal strifes. The populace lived in constant fear under the capricious rule of their king. In the midst of endless turbulent cruelty, there were brief periods of peace, when the kings who were otherwise occupied with their own lust for power and the security of their territory, dealt with civic and other duties of governance.

ABOVE:
The Gol Gumbaz has the distinction of being the largest dome built in the world. The architects and engineers patronized by the Adil Shahi dynasty fired the fervour for architecture in Bijapur and virtually reached for the sky in the construction of the Gol Gumbaz.

Municipal services consisted of little more than the provision of water to the city. In fact, just outside the city gates the soil of the countryside was ploughed up not by the tillers of land but by the cavalry and artillery of armies forever on the move.

It is evident by the lack of a town plan that Bijapur itself possessed no architects or planners of any merit. Among the learned men who attended the royal court were eminent *mohandis* and *mimars*, engineers and architects, who were commissioned to design the prominent buildings of the Adil Shahis and were persuaded to stay on, to build them under their own supervision. They fired the fervour for architecture in Bijapur and the builders were spurred on to virtually reach for the sky in the construction of the magnificent Gol Gumbaz.

Built in 1659 the Gol Gumbaz, was erected over the tomb of Sultan Mohammed, the seventh Adil Shahi ruler, who concentrated all his emotional and

RIGHT:
No camouflaged support was employed in the structure of the Gol Gumbaz thus proving the intelligence and effective management of the technique employed by the architects and the builders. The vast interior space of the Gumbaz is, however, lost within its own gloom, the somber darkness inside is appropriate for a tomb but disappointing for a visitor who is unable to see the architectural revelations of the structural techniques.

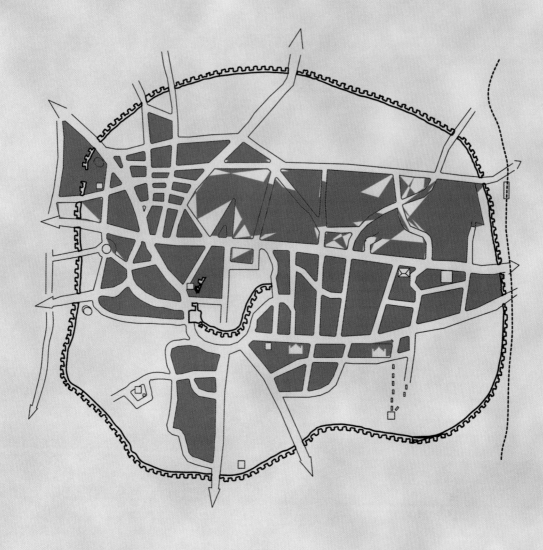

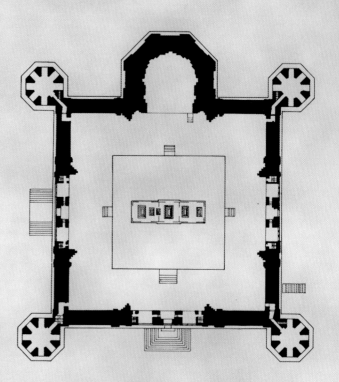

financial attention on building this colossal sepulchre for himself. The designer of the tomb was certainly a man of extraordinary ability and possessed of great structural skills and ideas. The dome is a very major work of its period and a symbol of the supreme structural triumph of Muslim builders anywhere in the world.

The dimensions of the dome speak for themselves. The plan is square, almost 41.5 metres (136 feet) inside and 62.5 metres (205 feet) from the outside. The four lofty walls are over 3 metres (10 feet) thick and 33.5 metres (110 feet) high; the diameter of octagonal buttresses is 7.6 metres (25 feet) rising to a height of 45.7 metres (150 feet); the hemispherical dome has a diameter of 44 metres (144 feet) on the outside and 38 metres (125 feet) inside; its apex is over 61 metres (200 feet) from ground level. Its height is the equivalent of a twenty-storeyed structure of modern times. This structure overshadows not only the low-rise urban skyline of the town, but many other monuments in the world by its sheer size as it is said to be the largest dome in the world. In a definitive way it is! Just as there are different ways to define the tallest building in the world there are also different criteria for measuring the size of a dome. A dome can be calculated as the largest either by its height, breadth and diameter or by the area covered by it. The Gol Gumbaz classifies as the largest dome in the world because the ground area covered by it is the largest, a distinctive achievement uniquely achieved.

The method of building a single dome over such a vast area was most intricate in technique and clearly visible in its manifestation. To build a dome, the western world used concealed devices like hidden iron chains girdling the base to prevent its splitting and hidden permanent scaffolding to support the arbitrary shape of an artificial non-structural dome. No such camouflaged support was employed in the structure of the Gol Gumbaz. The problem lay in supporting a circular dome over a large cubic space below and, even more pertinent, in intelligently managing the critical phase of conveyance. Conventionally, the Muslim builders had managed the transition through a lintel or by a series of pendentive or squinch arches that spanned across the corner of the square to create an octagon from which the spherical dome would spring. In a dome projected to the envisaged size of the Gol Gumbaz, the span across the corners of the square itself would have been 22.8 metres (75 feet) in width, which was well beyond the capabilities of existing techniques. Even if it could be achieved, the diameter of the dome would be so large that its structural load would have been twice that of the present dome. The problem then was to reduce the diameter of the base to a reasonable size and still retain the large square below. The mathematically learned *mohandis* solved this with great ingenuity by the creation of a smaller octagon in the larger square. This was achieved geometrically by twisting two concentric squares within the large square

intersecting with each other within the square producing a smaller octagon at the base from which the dome would rise. The designers invented the method of constructing 'intersecting arches'. On the ground, it involved the building of two arches springing from either of the square bases that would intersect below the apex of either, with the resulting fill in of masonry becoming the pudentrives that would hold up the dome. To counteract the huge load of the dome, the massive walls were buttressed with stolid and squat seven-storyed towers and the site chosen was such that the basement rested on solid rock just below the layer of earth on top.

The vast interior space thus created is, however, lost within its own gloom because it reflects only the dim light that penetrates its small openings, and illumines the floor that glimmers with a luminous softness. There is sombre darkness inside, appropriate for a tomb, but disappointing for the visitor who is unable to comprehend the architectural revelations of the structural techniques. Denied a view of its visual magnificence, the visitor can, however, indulge in the acoustic tricks of the 'whispering gallery' running at the base of the dome. The slightest murmur from any point in the gallery is heard from the other side as if the adjacent wall is talking back to you. The precise dimensions of the 'acoustic' gallery came about because of a structural necessity and the gallery is but an accidental result of its structural needs.

In the evening, from the terrace of the *Angur Mahal*, Sultan Mohammed must have often seen the dome of the sepulchre with the low western sun illuminating the building in a golden light. The Gumbaz would have been a flash of brilliant contrasting colour, with the mellow tints of its walls washed with a golden glow and the great dome shining like burnished brass. Today, the Sultan reposes peacefully in his huge mausoleum.

In 1720 A.D. a cloud was looming in the north that grew darker and brought with it a storm that carried everything before it. Aurangzeb at the head of the imperial Mughal army was marching southwards. The falcon was hard upon its prey, ready to make a final swoop on the city and once it struck, it left behind a mournful city, nevertheless picturesque in its beautiful buildings and its fine old tamarind and peepul trees. The shimmering views of the hoary ruins and the most perfect edifices were but a travesty of the once robust glories of Bijapur.

FACING PAGE:
The Gol Gumbaz was erected over the tomb of Sultan Mohammed, the seventh Adil Shahi ruler, who concentrated all his emotional and financial attention on constructing this colossal sepulchre for himself.

Padmanabhapuram

Feminine Timber

Kerala with its unique geography and culture is often hailed as 'god's own country'. Its tropical greenery is blessed by two annual monsoons and the climate is ideally suited for spice cultivation. The land has been sheltered from mainland invaders by the ghats, although its long coastline encouraged maritime contact with the outside world. The result is an interesting dichotomy between an eclectic exterior and a conservative interior. Connected like a network, Kerala's linear urban areas swell and thin out along its highways. These run parallel to the coast spanning over forty rivers that slice this part of the country into parallel strips of land joining the Western Ghats to the Arabian Sea. The roads, lanes, lagoons and the sea intersperse with one another, cutting through centres of habitation and the lush vegetation of palm, coconut and spice plantations.

Chera, its ancient name, was known to the Phoenician, Roman and Arab civilizations. The Maharajas of Travancore in the south (today, in the state of Tamil Nadu) enjoyed autonomous rule over the country of southern Kerala. They had built a large home for themselves in the countryside, and political compulsions gradually forced them to adopt it as their permanent residence. This house grew gradually over the years into a palace and was named Padmanabhapuram, or the 'City of the Lotus Born.' It was at its most splendid during the reign of Marthanda Verma Maharaj, a devotee of Lord Padmanabha, who christened the palace in A.D. 1744.

The boundary of this palace is not what a viewer would expect to see. A recently plastered wall, covered with a dull gray whitewash and a gateway that matches its drabness in colour, it looks more like the entrance to a bullpen. The entrance to the palace is just behind this dreary outer wall through the gate opening out into a quadrangular courtyard. Here, under a large tree that shades almost the entire area, are some jumbled pieces of cut rock weathered by the climate, and a few haphazardly placed stone benches. Lazy bulls, sleeping mongrels and agile cats loiter around feeding on the scraps thrown their way by the patrons of the cafeteria tucked away in a corner. The casual atmosphere of the courtyard where clothes are spread out to dry on the stones and benches makes one wonder if there really is a palace after all behind another intriguing wall in front.

The western wall facade displays tiled roofs, white plastered walls, timber balconies and a canopied entrance projecting into the courtyard. A gabled roofed pavilion houses a clock that has stopped working now, mute testimony to the vanished world of its erstwhile occupants. The main entry to the palace complex is through a high door on the first floor, with a pitched roof projecting over it. The

RIGHT:
The Maharajas of
Travancore built a large
home for themselves
in the countryside.
Political compulsions
made them adopt it as
their permanent
residence. The house
over the years grew into
a palace, and was called
Padmanabhapuram—
'City of the Lotus Born.'

RIGHT:
The western wall displaying tiled roofs, white plastered walls, timber balconies, and a canopied entrance projecting into the courtyard. A gabled roofed pavilion houses a clock.

BELOW:
Timber beams in a pyramidal formation hold up the gabled roof of the Padmanabhapuram Palace.

palace inside is deserted, but so well preserved that with a little imagination, one can visualize its royal residents who ruled over its temporal, residential and religious quadrants some two hundred years ago.

As part of the daily routine, royalty must have appeared in the morning on the balcony overlooking the courtyard to reassure the populace of their presence. The official meetings of the king took place in the *mantra shala* on the first floor of the structure, a level above the front quadrangle. Behind this lay the *upperika mallika,* the king's private prayer and rest rooms, which were accommodated in a four-storeyed structure. The topmost storey has a chamber furnished with a carved wooden bed for Lord Padmanabha to recline on. The bed is left symbolically empty but the walls are covered with paintings including a large portrait of the sleeping cosmic serpent.

The royal seat of the king, on display in the *mantra shala*, is fastidiously furnished, replicating as far as possible, the original throne, surrounded by the seats of ministers and nobility on exquisitely carved wooden benches, which were once covered with luxurious cushions. The benches ran just below its outer windows, masterpieces that display the ingenious craftsmanship of the local carpenters. The openings of the windows are filled with movable wooden louvres that can be held in any desired position by moving a single handle. They can be closed, half-opened or totally opened in keeping with the tropical climate of Kerala. When the monsoon rains come gushing down in the windy sweeps, not a drop of water passes through these delicate yet firm barriers. The openings are shaded by deep eaves supported on timber brackets fancifully shaped like the *vyali*, a mythical creature, which can take on the physical appearance of different animals.

Every object in the palace is saturated with a delicate touch. The fastidious hand of an influential female occupant is obvious. The women of Kerala, to date, have been exalted by its matriarchal society. It was the royal mother and her sisters who ruled the roost in all affairs of the court and surely it must have been the fastidious mind of the women that made Padmanabhapuram so unique among palaces. Through their efforts, they stressed that the palace was meant to be a home first and the king's seat of office next. Thus, they conveyed that the filial duties of the king were as important as his public duties.

The central zone of the palace houses the basic residential and official space occupied by the royal family. The core is the multi-storeyed *thai kottanam*, the

ABOVE:
Timber was lavishly used in the construction of Padmanabhapuram. The architecture and detailing, virtually of wood, are supremely elegant.

115

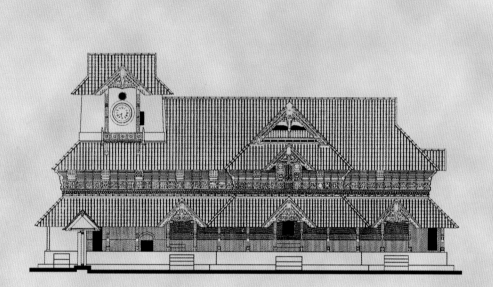

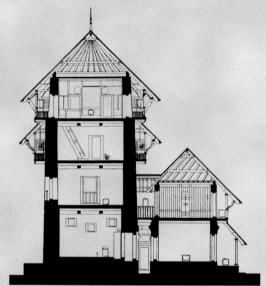

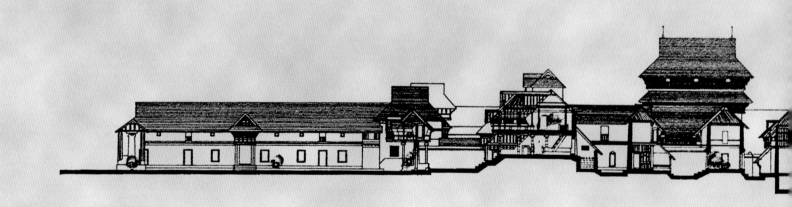

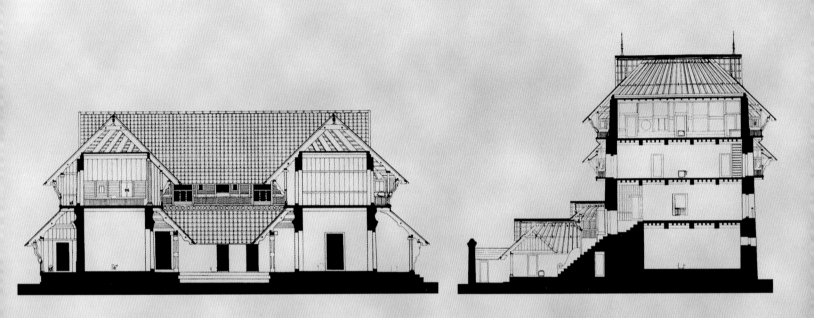

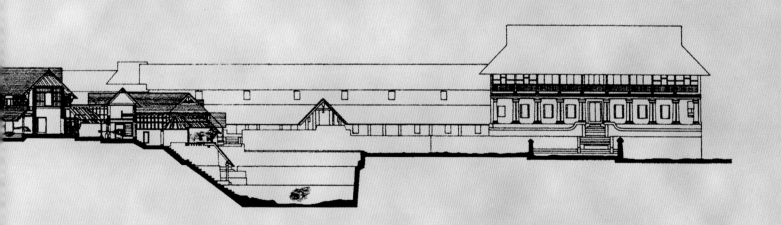

generic mother, on the upper floors, that contain the main living quarters of the kings and queens. The special bathing enclosure for royalty in the water tank was connected to the central enclosure through a maze of corridors to enable a private approach. Today, the water in the tank is infested by algae and is luminously green, but once it must have been crystal clear for a royal dip.

On the periphery of the zone of the kings, and defining its eastern, northern and southern boundaries are a series of oblong rectangular structures. These accommodate various ancillary functions such as the mint, weapons' store, the administrative and accounts offices of the palace, as well as various charity kitchens. An elaborate water drainage and sewage disposal system is laid sloping downwards to the southeast, in accordance with the rules of the *Vaastu Shastra*, the governing treatise on building in ancient India.

The structures were built with time-tested materials. Kerala is rich in timber, fine clay, laterite stone, granite and shell lime. Timber was used as fuel for baking tile and brick, while the walls were made of laterite, granite or brick or a combination of all three. As timber was lavishly used in the construction of this exquisite palace, naturally the place of pride was reserved for the carpenter's art. The most developed of the building crafts and sciences in Kerala, wood was the prime material preferred by the feminine rulers of the palace interiors. Its supremely elegant architecture is executed virtually with wood. There are rosewood ceilings carved in floral patterns, windows laid in with jewel-coloured mica and floors finished to a high polish and made with a special mix of crushed shells, lime, burnt coconuts husk, egg white amalgamated with the extracts of many local herbal plants. The result is a shining, mirror-like black floor.

ABOVE:
Stone pillars of the Navratri mandapam are carved with symbolic divine female figures and other motifs in relief. The small shrine is placed at the end of the long hall.

The 'sacred spaces' of the palace are discretely segregated from the residential and courtly quarters and located in the northern periphery. This ensured that they could be utilized for public functions and also afford privacy for royal ladies who wanted to attend the functions. One of these is the *nataka shala*, the theatre of classical dance directly interlinked with the *mantra shala* to enable royalty or courtiers to participate conveniently in any function. The other temple for exclusively religious celebrations was called the Navratri mandapam and was built in conformity with the ancient Indian tradition of stone. The stone pillars of the mandapam are carved with symbolic divine female figures and other decorative motifs in relief. A small shrine is placed at the end of a long hall and a delicate structure in timber, shaded by wooden screens with peeping windows, is for seating female royalty in seclusion.

How has such a lovely palace survived to date almost in the condition as it was when built? In all probability Padmanabhapuram was nurtured by its ongoing

maritime contact with the east and the west. It also did not die a sudden calamitous death, but merely languished into retirement.

Possibly, the security officers at the gate do the visitors a favour by charging an exorbitant fee at the gate for allowing sketching equipment, cameras and video cameras to be carried in. For the charming, delectable architectural delicacies of the palace set amidst the lingering fragrance of rosewood are better treasured in the memory.

ABOVE:
Furnished colonnaded hall showing the obvious fastidious touch of a female occupant. The status of women in Kerala has been exalted by the mores of a matriarchal system, prevalent even to date.

Ground Plan of Padmanabhapuram Palace

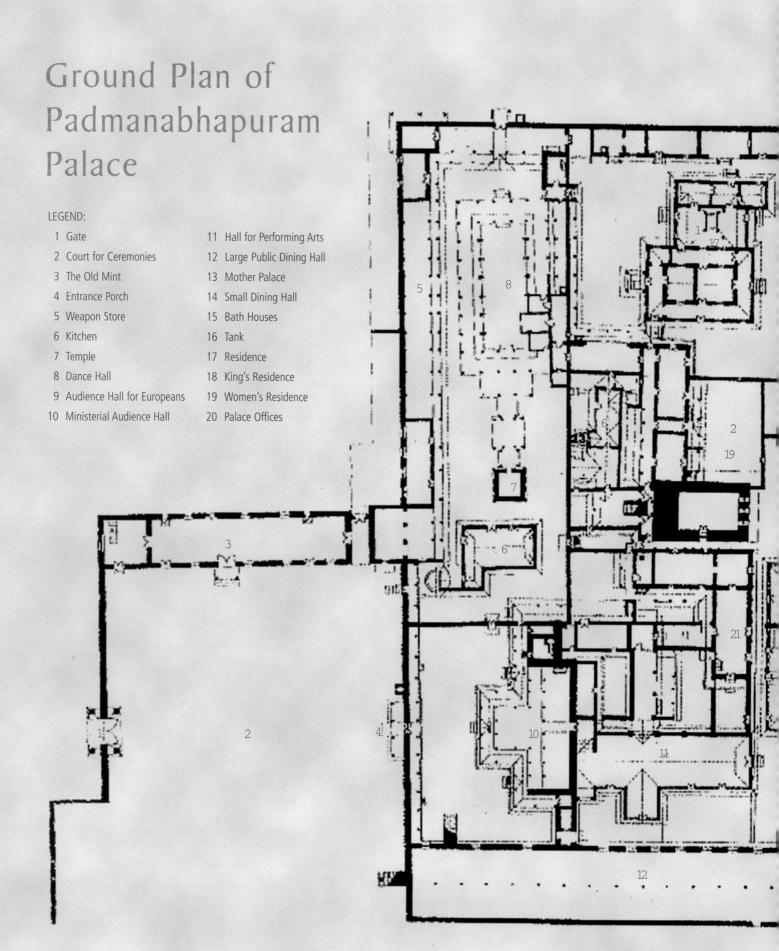

LEGEND:

1	Gate	11	Hall for Performing Arts
2	Court for Ceremonies	12	Large Public Dining Hall
3	The Old Mint	13	Mother Palace
4	Entrance Porch	14	Small Dining Hall
5	Weapon Store	15	Bath Houses
6	Kitchen	16	Tank
7	Temple	17	Residence
8	Dance Hall	18	King's Residence
9	Audience Hall for Europeans	19	Women's Residence
10	Ministerial Audience Hall	20	Palace Offices

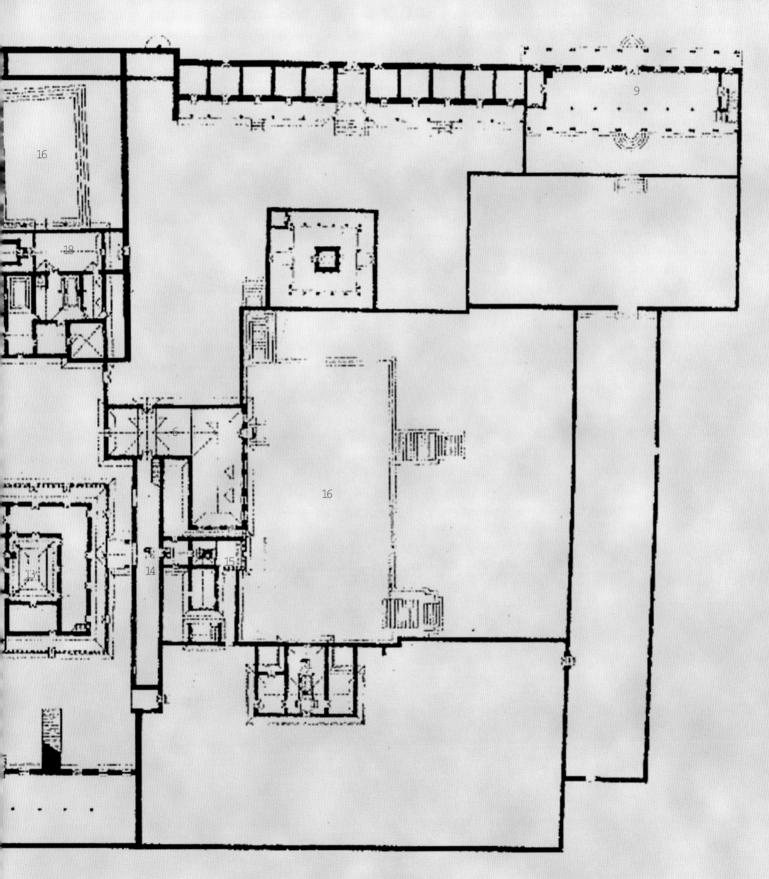

LEFT:
The shimmering reflective black floor of the hall is a result of finishing with a high polish made of a special mix of crushed shells, lime, burnt coconut husk, egg white, mixed with the extracts of many local herbal plants.

Jaisalmer

Curved in Sand

The road to Jaisalmer through the Thar Desert seems to lead nowhere. The interminable repetitiveness of the desert, flat and monotonously brown, is quilted with patches of thorny yellow bushes and cactus clusters. There is no sign of life anywhere and nothing moves except for the sand dunes with their ripples of loose sand rising and falling in waves. There is only ceaseless heat and the fierce light of the sun. The barren ridges and the shifting *teebas* of sand are the only features that stand out in the uniform flatness of the region. No wonder a desert folk song says:

> *Ghee dhule tho maharo*
> *Kachu nahin bigade*
> *Panni dhule tho maharo*
> *Jiyo jal jai*
>
> If ghee is wasted
> That is no loss,
> If water is wasted
> My very being is lost.

What was once a narrow camel trail is now a solid tarmac road. But on stepping off the road, one's ankles sink into a quagmire of loose sand. There are signboards that indicate that one is about to cross over from a 'rare cultivation' zone to a more fearsome one of 'positive sterility'. Then suddenly, the hazy image of a seemingly battered ocean liner looms up from the vast barren expanse: a *'Sonar Qilla'* arises large like a dream conjured from a wasteland of rock and sand. This is Jaisalmer, a huge fortification at world's end.

Doubtless, the earliest known ruler of Jaisalmer must have been a rare visionary to conceive and build such a fantasy in stone. The capital of the *Bhattis,* desert feudal chiefs and leaders, was situated in the country known to ancient Indian geographers as *Marusthali,* the place of death, but Jaisalmer is built on the edge of the Gadisar Lake, a rain-fed pond from which potable water was drawn under the watchful eye of the *Rawal* himself who ensured an equitable distribution of this precious commodity.

On the advice of a local hermit Eesul, the *Bhatti* King Maharawal Jaisal abandoned his fort at Lodurva to found the city in A.D. 1156 on the *Trikuta* Hill, an outcrop of the Aravalli range. His successors claimed descent from the *Yadu*

ABOVE:
Salim Singh's haveli
in which the lower
floors are
conventional but
the upper portion
projects out boldly.
The ship-like
eminence of this
floor contains the
residences of his
concubines. The
haveli reaches to a
height almost equal
to the adjacent
walls of the fort.

kings who ruled from the Yamuna to the 'world's end.' They built an enormous wall with ninety-nine bastions around the original fort and within it constructed a city protected from the shifting sands of the desert and also from the attacks of neighbouring tribes. The *Bhattis* were feudal chiefs and leaders of fearsome brigands renowned for their armed skills. They earned wealth for the city from taxes they levied on trade and traders who passed through the city. In return, they provided security to the caravans that halted at Jaisalmer when going along the ancient spice route that cut across the desert. However, they were constantly engaged in war with the other desert tribes. Out of this incessant friction, there emerged a history of intrigue, treachery, abduction and murder that could only take place in the fevered heat of a simmering, isolated desert stronghold.

The fort stretches across a hill more than 250 feet high, 1500 feet long, and a 750 feet wide man-made plateau with the township laid out on the plain below, as a section of a circle on the eastern periphery of the fort. Parallel to the circumference of the fort in the middle of the city is a broad bazaar accommodating shops and workplaces. The rest of the area is residential and threaded together by roads, lanes and by-lanes. Keeping in mind the inconsistent availability of water, the unmerciful heat and the severe desert winters, its

RIGHT:
A view of the Durbar
Court in Jaisalmer Fort.

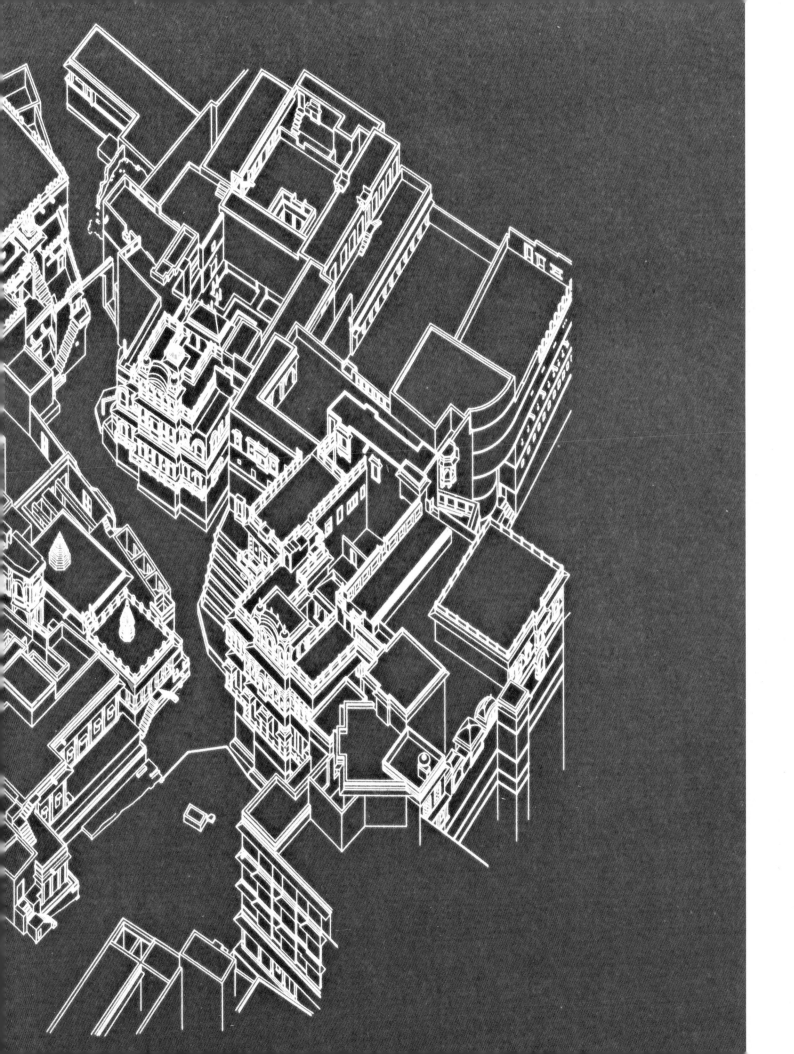

planners and architects built the city to respond precisely to the geographic and climatic conditions of the region.

The houses and havelis in the residential areas are planned on a uniform pattern. All dwellings were built around an open-to-sky courtyard, which was the

core of the house. It induced a funnel-like convection current that sucked the hot air upwards to ventilate the house. On the ground floor were the kitchen, lavatory, bath and a room or rooms depending on the size of the house. The houses of the affluent were built over a basement, which offered a cool retreat in the summer and a warm abode in the winter. A staircase ascended from the courtyard to additional rooms on the upper floor. The houses of the rich businessmen, bureaucrats and courtiers were even higher so that they could catch the cool evening winds in the summer. The street side elevations of the houses displayed the wealth of the occupants for while the houses of the commoners were decorated minimally, the multi-storeyed havelis of the affluent were panelled with exquisitely and richly carved soft yellow desert sandstone.

The three most prominent havelis belonged to *Nathmalji* and the *Patwa*, affluent traders and moneylenders, and to Salim Singh, an influential courtier. The *Nathmal* haveli belonged to two brothers who built adjoining havelis, with facades designed by two different master builders who were instructed to make them symmetrical but not identical. A tall order indeed! However, the master builders responded brilliantly and executed their clients' orders to perfection. To the trained eye, there were differences in the details of the brackets, *chajjas* and *jaalis* but the broad framework of the *Bengal* canopies that shaded all the balconies was symmetrical. Salim Singh's haveli is different from the others in that the lower floors are conventional but the upper portion projects out boldly. The ship-like eminence of this floor contains the residences of his concubines. The haveli reaches to a height almost equal to the adjacent walls of the fort, from where it is said, Salim Singh intended to build a bridge across the wall to the royal palace. This was intended as a challenge to royalty and was prohibited by protocol.

Today, students of architecture and planning scout the streets, lanes and by-

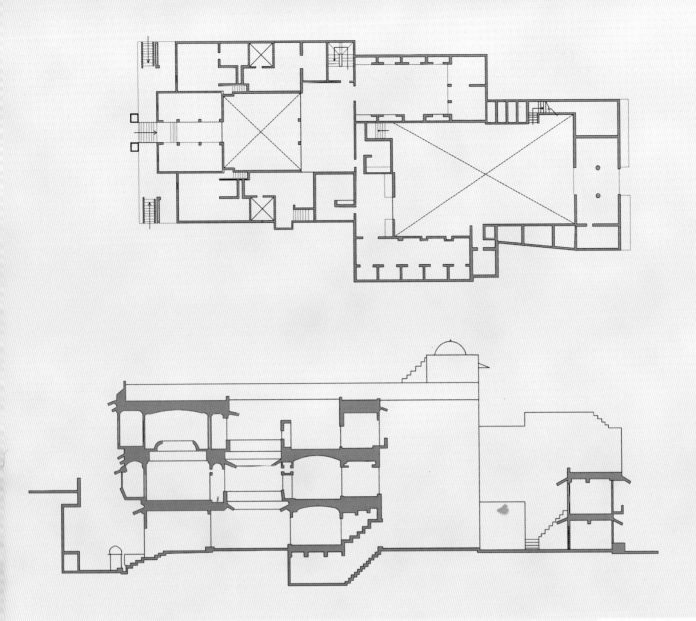

lanes of Jaisalmer and enter a deserted house to carry out detailed studies to understand how the principles of planning produced such a viable answer to the peculiar problems of the desert. Several architects have written doctoral theses on the subject of passive cooling methods in the desert employed by the builders of Jaisalmer.

The *Palliwal* Brahmans, who strangely enough lived a semi-agricultural life despite their high caste, were one of the power centres to contend with in the politics of Jaisalmer. They were temporal proprietors of Palli and all its lands long before the *Rathors*, a clan of warrior Rajputs, colonized Marwar, and built large suburban settlements in the desert around the city. Their houses are a lavish rural version of the dwellings of the urbanites. These houses had a large courtyard surrounded by a generous pen for animals, with many rooms located on the ground level and an occasional first-floor room attached to the terrace used for sleeping at night. Many of the orderly townships of the *Palliwals* have survived and remain unscathed by the passage of time. At one time the *Palliwals* fell out

ABOVE:
Plan and section of
Nathmal ki Haveli.

FACING PAGE:
The houses of the affluent were built over a basement, which offered a cool retreat in the summer and a warm abode in the winter. A staircase ascended from the courtyard to additional rooms on the upper floor.

with Salim Singh on state matters and with typical Brahmanical pride evacuated all the townships and departed en masse with their cattle and households, never to return. They also left a large vacuum in the economy of the city-state. One of these towns and a large area around it has been preserved and surrounded by a wired fence by the Archaeological Survey of India and is proclaimed a Heritage Township today.

Another fragile heritage that survives is the distinctive attire of the shepherds of the region, which is fashioned to suit the desert climate. James Todd describes it as 'a *jamah*, or tunic of white cloth or chintz reaching to the knee; the cummerbund, or couture, tied so high as to present no appearance of waist, very loose trousers in many folds, drawn tight at the ankles, and a turban, generally of a scarlet colour, rising conically a full foot from the head. The women favour the *chaori*, rings of ivory or bone, with which they cover their arms from the shoulder to the wrist.' The tribal women had a more economical and sensual attire. For a blouse they adopted a backless *choli*, which is tied by a thin string or strings around the neck, back and waist holding the breasts within its small frontal piece. With the *choli* is worn the traditional heavily pleated *ghaghra* (full skirt). The whole costume is brightly coloured, embroidered and embellished with small pieces of glass sewn in intricate designs on the hem of the skirt and the *choli*. In place of the turban the women cover their heads with a long *chunari*.

ABOVE:
A tumultuous aggregation of canopies all in yellow desert sandstone.

The edges of the fort precincts are dotted with many ancient Jain temples dating from the twelfth to the fifteenth centuries, which were lavishly covered with sculptures inspired by Jain mythology. Towards the right of the mandapam of the Rishbadevji Temple, the austere images of Jain *tirthankaras* are seen sitting in meditation in a circle. The temples were built with the donations of wealthy *Marwaris* and are built of the same material as the fort and the city within. Their architecture merges into the walls and battlements of the fort and the scene comprises one enormous tableau. It is a tumultuous aggregation of canopies, latticed balconies and galleries—all in the yellow desert sandstone. The king's living quarter was a complex consisting of three distinct palaces: one for his official work, one for his queen and another for his concubines. The *zenanas* of the palace seem gloomy at first sight, but suddenly open out into courtyards decorated with latticed screens and tier upon tier of carved balconies. Because the *Bhattis* were *Chandravanshis* or descendents of the moon, the furniture in the palace was exclusively of silver, the colour closest to the moon's radiance.

The Maharaja of Baroda observes that 'Jaisalmer has always loitered around the margin of Rajput history and has for the most part been spared the travails of the other Rajput states to the west.' But history finally caught up with the *Jaisals* too. The *Bhatti* rajas became subordinate to the Mughals in the late seventeenth century. In December 1818, the *Bhattis* were the last of the Rajput princes forced to make a treaty with the British. Before the arrival of the British, the ruler had allowed the post of prime minister to become hereditary and two royal dynasties were poisoning one another with monotonous regularity leaving the deck open for the British to play their political card.

For a long time after the British left, Jaisalmer remained a ghost town. The railway station was a shed over a non-existent platform, and the bus stop, a tin depot with hardly any arrivals and departures. The main market was merely a small chowk where basic goods, from vegetables to toys, cloth, sweets and imitation jewellery were sold. Anyone could walk its deserted streets and lanes and enter with impunity into any of its many vacant and unlocked houses.

However, the king held virtual mock courts in his palace and received meagre *nazranas* ranging from eight annas to a rupee or two from the tribes loyal to the king till as late as the 1960s. The Maharaja made it a point to come from Delhi to claim his due to preserve the traditional customs and his rights to property. But today, Jaisalmer has been discovered by tourists, both domestic and foreign—French, English, German, Japanese. South and North Indian restaurants and inns abound in the crowded streets and bustling *gallis*. Rich merchants selling exotic handicrafts have taken over the houses and converted them into commercial establishments. The palace and the large centrally located havelis have become 'Heritage Hotels', both mock and genuine. The town today is dressed up like a fairy queen in the 'Land of Death.'

ABOVE:
A *Sonar Qilla* arises large like a dream conjured from a wasteland of rock and sand. This is Jaisalmer, a huge fortification at world's end.

Taj Mahal

Phantasmal Perfection

As the sun rises over the city of Agra, it caresses the domes and minarets of the Taj Mahal with its warm effulgence coaxing the monument to reveal its ethereal beauty to the world. However, on a full moon night the communion between the Taj Mahal and the moon is truly cosmic. The night sky seems illumined by two moons, the orb in the sky and the dome of the Taj Mahal set aglow by the lunar light. Against an ink-blue sky with its immense sieve of blue stars the softly illumined mass of the Taj Mahal dissolves into a floating vision. For every change of light, in winter or summer, the Taj Mahal displays a new facet of its beauty. In Agra, whether seen from across the railway lines or from the flat dry rural countryside, through the oriels of the fort or even from behind the sooty chimneys of factories, the Taj Mahal appears a glorious beacon of beauty.

The fifth Mughal Emperor Shah Jahan created this architectonic wonder in A.D. 1560 to keep alive the memory of his beloved queen, Arjumand Banu, royally titled Mumtaz Mahal. She was the most beloved of all his wives who had died giving birth to their fourteenth child. It seems as if she arose momentarily from her makeshift grave and whispered into the emperor's ear a description of the heavenliness of the other world. In building the Taj Mahal the emperor apparently recreated her perception of heaven and the 'Garden of Paradise', which he laid out at the feet of the queen's last resting place, creating on earth an architectural paradigm of the entire gamut of Islam's perception of life and the afterworld.

That Shah Jahan had savoured much of the promised joys of paradise on earth is borne out by rumours rife in court about the youthful prince's sexual peccadilloes. In his old age, however, he became a pious Muslim and observed all the rituals of Islam. At the same time he also became obsessed with the idea of his unique place in history. Throughout his life, Shah Jahan strove to emulate and surpass the heroic building deeds of his grandfather Akbar. In fact, as a favourite grandchild, he must have been an ardent listener at the sessions on architecture that his grandfather held when he built Fatehpur Sikri in red sandstone and later to his father Jahangir when he was building the Itmad-ud-Dulah in pure white marble. Architecture seemed to have been in his blood and he expressed his

132

passion through beautiful buildings, for he knew that their glory alone would earn him a permanent place in history. He expressed the vision of his grandfather in red sandstone and his father in white marble, and built monuments as enduring memorials to his own greatness. He was not only a passionate but also a prolific builder and during his reign had built mosques, palaces and forts. Above all, he laid out a new city, the seventh city of Delhi, the eponymous Shahjahanabad. The crowning glory of his abiding passion, however, was the Taj Mahal, the most opulent masterpiece of architecture in the world.

To build the Taj Mahal, Shah Jahan wanted the best talent available in the country, and to unearth it, he floated what could today be termed an 'architectural competition' to seek the concepts of the renowned architects of the times. The ultimate winner, in principle, was the proposal from Ustad Ahmed of Lahore. However, this concept was translated into reality under the strict aesthetic

ABOVE:
The Taj Mahal with its surrounding, formally planned Mughal garden that lends to the ethereal ambience.

FACING PAGE:
A tomb intricately decorated with inlay work and pietra dura that depicts flowers drooping gracefully as if paying homage to those buried within.

supervision of Shah Jahan himself. What Ustad Ahmed had presented to the emperor evoked memories of the Chahar Bagh in Isfahan, glimpses of the Tomb of Timur in Samarkand, and the four-corner minarets of the Char Minar at Tabriz. A fusion of derivatives from well-known masterpieces, the Taj Mahal was presented as a unified entity and 'an apt combination of rich sobriety, amplitude, and sedate proportions.' Begley wrote in his anthology on the monument: 'The Taj is an ideal and complete work of human architecture. The complex clearly stands as the logical culmination of the earlier Mughal architectural tradition (imbibing traditional Hindu and Buddhist notions), combining bold engineering and massive scale with formal elegance and a totally coordinated design of flawless visual symmetry.' This is the ultimate and most precise architectural and structural account of the Taj Mahal.

Naturally, many poetic and graphic accounts also abound. 'The Taj mirrors the

passing colours and moods of every moment, from the soft dreaminess of dawn and the dazzling whiteness at midday to when it is softly illuminated by the brief Indian afterglow to assume the enchanting tint of some pale and lovely rose,' wrote Gascoine in *The Great Mughals*. An Italian traveller registers it as a spasm of pain—'the beauty of Taj invested in me in such a violent cutting short of my word and my breath.' To one viewer, it appeared to be a 'cloud reclined upon an airy throne', and to another, 'a vision of grief turned into a glacial calm.' A contemporary Urdu poet Sahir Ludhianvi beseeched his beloved not to meet him at the Taj Mahal, since Shah Jahan had mocked their humble love by building such an ostentatious offering to his beloved. And on a moonlit night, Tagore, the poet-laureate of India, says it becomes 'the tear on the face of eternity.'

Every aspect of the Taj Mahal—its landscape, colour, decoration and spatial or architectonic qualities—has been meticulously coordinated. Unlike other mausoleums of Mughal royalty that were planted in the centre of a formal garden, the Taj Mahal stands proudly at the head of one. On the other end the waters of the Yamuna rise and fall against its huge stylobate. When the river is a narrow placid stream, the Taj Mahal seems to rise out of the sand dunes of the riverbed, and when the river is abundant, its waters mirror its beauty. The Taj Mahal stands like the guardian of a perfect ecological cycle. The grand lawns that surround it today were at one time orchards of fruit and aromatic plants, which were nourished by the high water table created by the river. Wells were dug in the south and the water drawn from them would irrigate the orchards and feed the strategically located pools of water that became integral to the disciplined lawns of grass later planted by the British and bordered by cypress trees.

The size of the monument is revealing. The entire conception is contained within a north-south aligned rectangle measuring 1900 ft x 1000 ft (579.2m x 304.8 m). On the southern side is located a square garden of 1000 ft. (304.8 m) side. The complex is enclosed within a high boundary wall with broad octagonal pavilions at each corner. The main monument itself stands on a square, 187 ft (57 m) on all sides and a 22 ft. (6.7m) high platform and has a basement where the body of Mumtaz Mahal is enshrined. You have to descend to an underground encrypt to see the actual grave, a facsimile of which exists on the ground floor.

The form of the Taj Mahal is composed of pure volumes. It is a perfectly chamfered cuboid pierced by stately robust arches that give way to a bulbous dome, derived from a perfect sphere. The dome of the Taj Mahal is flanked by four similarly roofed *chattaries* at the corners. The composition becomes a facile grouping, rhythmically disposed and skilfully interrelated with each part in its total unity. The cuboid rests symmetrically on a massive square stylobate, at each corner of which is planted an elegant minaret. On two sides of the monument are two perfectly alike structures, one a mosque on the west, and its architectural *jawaab* literally meaning reply, the *mehman khana* or the V.I.P. guesthouse on the east.

The Ground Floor Plan

The Taj Mahal is a glorious culmination of the artistic fusion of Indian architecture and Mughal ornamentation. It was built over a period of twenty-two years (1632–54), with a labour force of approximately 20,000 workers, at a monumental cost that has never been precisely tabulated. The work was supervised by experienced architects like Makramat Khan and Mir Abdul Karim, though there can be no doubt that the ultimate vision and guidance was Shah Jahan's alone.

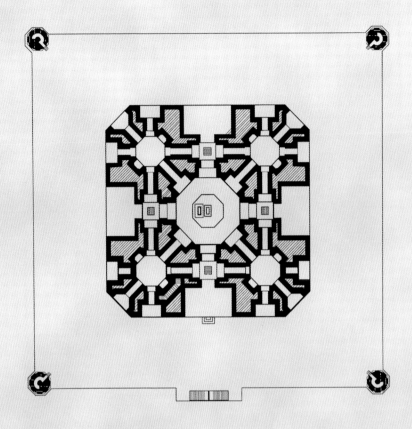

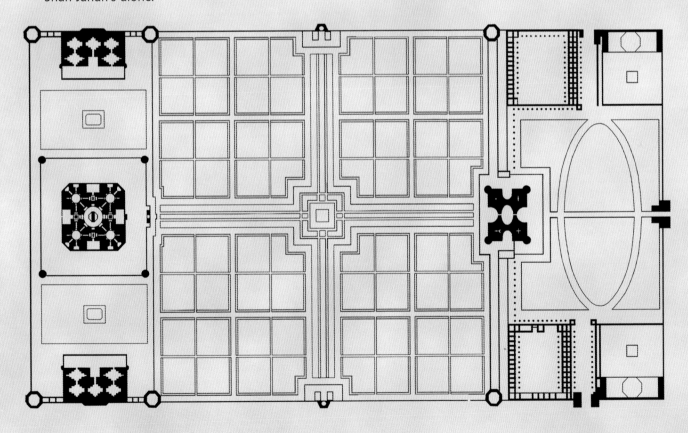

LEFT:
A breathtakingly unusual view of the Taj Mahal from across the river. The waters of the Yamuna ebb and flow against its huge stylobate. When the river is in spate its waters mirror its beauty. When it falls, the Taj Mahal seems to rise out of the river bed. The Taj Mahal stands like the guardian of a perfect ecological cycle.

The plain marble surface inside and outside the Taj Mahal was tempered with inlays of pearls and other precious stones through the exquisite technique of pietra dura. The panels at the base were filled with delicately sculpted images of flowers. The relief panels at the base of the main arches were also bordered by lengths of inlaid calligraphy, the size of the vertical inscription calibrated so that in perspective they appear constant from below.

BELOW: A section of the dome and main building of the Taj Mahal.

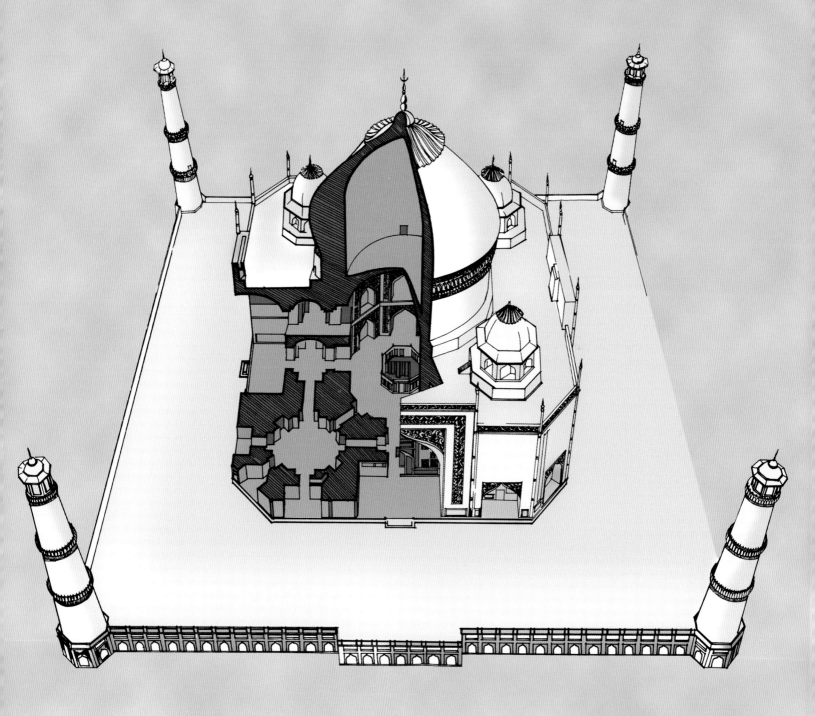

In plan, the Taj Mahal adopts the *pancharatna* plan of Hindu temples wherein the central deity is supported by four subordinate ones at each corner. In the Taj Mahal the dome is the centrepiece supported by four *chattries* at each corner. Its language, however, is resolutely Islamic, displaying forms of pristine arches, domes and minarets.

The Taj Mahal may appear to be a fantasy building but it is planned on a mathematically perfect and geometrical system. The subtly deceptive techniques and the Taj Mahal's blatant revelation of these is a testament to the contemporaneity of the work. The clarity of this process is a tribute to the timeless architectural genius behind the Taj Mahal. Can one really dare to explain the subtle skills employed by the architect, or would it be sacrilegious to demystify the architecture of the Taj Mahal? The technicalities truly beggar description.

On first view, the Taj Mahal fits snugly within the formal entrance gate. This frame provides no references to any familiar features leaving the viewer clueless about the actual size of the building. Even the umbilical connection between the earth and the Taj Mahal is absent, as the stairway leading up to the edifice is hidden from view, shrouded as it is within the fold of its walls.

The 220 feet high Taj Mahal is equivalent to that of a twenty-storyed contemporary building but in fact the monument appears to be two-storyed, since the elevation is constituted of a large central arch flanked on either side of two superimposed rows of arches. Further, the architecturally ungainly structural necessity of a drum on which the bulbous dome rests is masked from view by an articulated parapet. The whole is in reality a perpetually abstract camouflage achieved through several architectural manipulations.

The Taj Mahal is panelled with glowing white marble, which if left bare, would blind one by the reflection of the rays of the sun. The marble's plain surface was tempered with inlays of pearls and other precious stones through the exquisite technique of pietra dura. The panels at the base were filled with delicately sculpted images of rose bushes drooping their heads gracefully as if to salute the empress who was buried within. Lengths of inlaid calligraphy, the size of the vertical inscription duly calibrated so that in perspective they appear constant from below, bordered these relief panels at the base and the main arches.

Viewed as a classical monument, the Taj Mahal transcends the boundaries of architectural definition. Just as Urdu reached its ultimate fruition in the poetry of Ghalib who fused Hindu theology and Islamic ideas with unsurpassed lucidity, the Taj Mahal represents the pinnacle of architecture in India, a century before the poetry of Ghalib reached a peak in Urdu literature. Does architecture really herald ideas before literature gives them spoken expression? The Taj Mahal seems to suggest so.

Glossary

Aankh mei chauli: hide and seek

Ajivikas: a sect of the Jain monks in the Barabar Hills

Alai Darwaza: an entrance hall with a gate

Antralaya: anteroom

Ardh mandapam: hall preceding the main mandapam

Bhima: an elongated barrel-shaped hall

Bhog Mandir: a hall for the gods to bless the food offered by donors for distribution to the destitute

Buland Darwaza: Victory Gate

Chaitya halls: halls that contain a stupa

Chattra: an umbrella of protection

Chajjas: eves

Chaori: rings of ivory or bone

Chaupat court: chess-like game

Choli: small blouse worn with a *ghaghara* or sari

Choultry: large hall with columns

Chunari: veil

Daftar Khanna: secretariat

Dargah: tomb

Darshan: audience

Darwaza: gate

Diwan-i-Aam: hall of public audience

Diwan-i-Khas: hall of private audience

Devadasis: girls dedicated to the deity

Deul: inner cella

Dharmaraja: a full form of the south Indian *vimana* type temple

Gallies: streets

Garbh griha: sanctum sanctorum

Ghaghra: full pleated ankle-length skirt

Ghungroos: ankle bells

Gopurams: pyramidal towers

Ilahi-gaz: Mughal measure

Jaalies: lattice work

Jagmohan: hall facing the cella

Jamah: loose pyjamas that taper at the ankles

Jawaab: reply

Jhopra: rustic structure in stone

Jinas: teachers

Kalyan Mandapam: wedding hall

Khajur: the date palm tree

Khwabgah: sleeping quarters

Lats of Ashoka: the message of Buddha carved on stone tablets and located at strategic points

Liwan: roofed portion of the mosque

Lungi: a long piece of unstitched cloth worn by males

Mahavira: the last and the most revered teacher of Jainism

Mantra shala: official hall of the king
Marwari: merchants
Masjid: a place of prostration
Mehman khanna: guesthouse
Mehrab: holy arch in the middle of the *liwan*
Mimars: architects
Minars: spires of Islamic architectural style
Mohandis: engineers

Nat Mandir: hall for dance performances
Nataka shala: theatre of classical dance
Nazranas: tributes

Odissi: classical dance form of Orissa

Palaki: palanquin
Panch Mahal: palace of five inwardly
   receding storeys
Pancharatna: five jewels
Parikramas: circumambulatory path
Pradakshina: circumambulatory path
Pyaadas: chess pieces

Rauza: mixed structure containing a tomb
   and a mosque
Rawal: king

Sonar Qilla: Golden Fort
Shikharas: temple spires

Stambhas: pillars
Sworannapushp kandini: the tank of the
   golden lilies

Teebas: hilltops
Thai kottanam: the generic mother
Tirthankaras: teachers
Toranas: free standing decorated gateways
Trikuta: triangular

Urusringas: shikharas in relief
Upperika mallika: the king's private prayer
   and rest rooms

Vaastu Shastra: the governing treatise on
   building in ancient India.
Vaayu: air
Vedika: railing reminiscent of the transition
   from wood to stone
Vidyadevis: goddesses of knowledge
Vimana: to measure
Vyali: a mythical creature, which can take
   on the physical appearance of different
   animals

Yakshinis: gatekeepers

Zenanas: living quarters of women

Bibliography

Basham, A.L., *The Wonder that was India*, Sidgwick & Jackson, London, 1954.

Batley, C., *Design Development of Indian Architecture*, John Murray, London, 1934.

Brown, P., *Indian Architecture (Buddhists and Hindu Period)*, Taraporevala & Sons, Bombay, 1965.

Brown, P., *Indian Architecture (Islamic Period)*, Taraporevala & Sons, Bombay, 1942.

Burgess, J., *Muhammadan Architecture in Gujarat*, Indological Book House, Varanasi, 1971.

Cousens, H., *Bijapur and Its Architectural Remains*, Bharatiya Publishing House, Varanasi, 1976.

Croness and Haywoods, *The Gardens of Mughal India*, Vikas, New Delhi, 1973.

Cunningham, A., *Archaeological Survey of India*, Vols. I–XXIII, Simla, Calcutta, 1903–30.

Edwardes, M., *Indian Temples and Palaces*, Paul Hamlyn, London, 1959.

Fergusson, J., *History of Indian & Eastern Architecture*, John Murray, London, 1910.

Goetz, H., *Five Thousand Years of Indian Art*, Methuen, London, 1959.

Hambly, G., *Cities of Moghul India*, Vikas, New Delhi, 1977.

Havell, E.B., *The Ancient and Medieval Architecture of India*, John Murray.

Havell. E.B., *The Ideals of Indian Art*, John Murray, London, 1920.

Jairazbhoy, R.A., *An Outline of Islamic Architecture*, Asia Publishing House, Bombay, 1921.

Kramrisch, S., *The Hindu Temple*, University of Calcutta Press, Calcutta, 1946.

Lal, K., *Temples and Sculptures of Bhubaneswar*, Arts & Letters, New Delhi, 1970.

Majumdar, R.C., (Ed.), *The Delhi Sultanate*, Bharatiya Vidya Bhawan, Bombay, 1960.

Majumdar, R.C., Raychaudhuri, M.C., Datta, K., *Advanced History of India*, Macmillan, London, 1963.

Marshall, J., *Annual Reports of the Archaeological Survey of India*, Calcutta, 1903–30.

Marshall, J., *Mohenjodaro and the Indus Civilization*, London, 1931.

Michell, G., (Ed.), *Architecture of the Islamic World,* Thames, Hudson, London, 1978.

Nehru, J., *The Discovery of India*, Meridian Books, London, 1946.

Piggot, S., *Pre-historic India*, Penguin Books, Harmondsworth, 1950.

Rawlinson, H.G., *India, A Short Cultural History*, The Cresset Press, London, 1937.

Rowland, B., *The Art and Architecture of India*, Penguin Books, Harmondsworth, 1953.

Spear, P., *A History of India*, Vol. 2, Penguin Books, Baltimore, 1965.

Thapar, R., *A History of India*, Penguin Books, Harmondsworth, 1966.

Volwahsen, A., *Living Architecture of India*, MacDonald, London, 1970.

Volwahsen, A., *Living Architecture, Islamic-Indian,* Macdonald, London, 1970.

Wheeler, R.E.M., *Early India and Pakistan*, Thames and Hudson, London, 1959.

Wheeler, R.E.M., *The Indus Civilization*, Cambridge University Press, Cambridge, 1953.

Zimmer, H., *The Art of Indian Asia*, Oxford University Press, London, 1968.

Photo Credits

Balan M

4 (bottom row from left: third, 113, 114 (top),
115, 118, 119, 122-123, Back cover

B P S Walia

23

MD Sharma

61, 63

Prakash Israni

4 (top row from left: first), 16-17, 21, 31,
34-35, 36, 64-65, 68, 71, 76-77

Roli Books

Front cover, 1, 4 (top row from left: second, third, fourth;
bottom row from left: first, second, fourth); centre;
5 (top row from left: first, second [J.L. Nou], third; bottom),
6, 8-9, 10, 11, 38-39, 41, 42-43, 45, 47, 49, 61, 63, 72-73, 74,
91, 95, 98-99, 102-103, 106-107, 125, 128, 130, 131, 132,
133, 134, 136-137, 139

Satish Grover

14-15, 56 and all the line drawings

Toby Sinclair

2-3, 5 (top row from left: fourth), 13, 25, 28-29, 42-43, 46, 50, 51,
52-53, 55, 57, 58-59, 80-81, 82-83, 84, 86, 87, 89, 105, 110-111